STAMP COLLECTING

An illustrated guide and handbook for adult collectors

BARRY KRAUSE

BETTERWAY PUBLICATIONS, INC.
WHITE HALL, VIRGINIA

Published by Betterway Publications, Inc.
P.O. Box 219
Crozet, VA 22932
(804) 823-5661

Cover design by Deborah B. Chappell
Typography by Park Lane Associates

Much of the material in this book originally appeared in the author's column, "Your Stamps," in the *Los Angeles Times* from 1982 to 1989. The material has been updated to reflect the current stamp market and subsequently discovered information.

All photographs were taken by the author of philatelic items in his own collection.

Library of Congress Cataloging-in-Publication Data

Krause, Barry
    Stamp collecting : an illustrated guide and handbook for adult collectors / Barry Krause
       p.   cm.
    Bibliography: p.
    Includes index.
    ISBN: 1-55870-127-3 : $9.95
    1. Postage-stamps--Collectors and collecting--Handbooks, manuals, etc. 2. Postage-stamps--Collectors and collecting--Miscellanea.
I. Title.
HE6215.K725   1989
769.56'075--dc20
                                      89-36136
                                         CIP

Printed in the United States of America
0 9 8 7 6 5 4 3 2

To my parents, Leonard J. and Helen Krause,
who gave me something more precious than stamps:
a happy and secure childhood!

ACKNOWLEDGMENTS

The *Los Angeles Times* and Times Mirror Co. — for allowing me to reprint excerpts from my column "Your Stamps" which has appeared in the *Times* since 1982. Much of this book is based on my column which follows a question-and-answer format from questions sent to the *Times* by readers.

Bobbie Justice, Editor of the "You Section" of the *Times*, and my stamp column.

Kodak Processing Laboratory of Hollywood, CA — for film developing of the photo negatives.

Super Color Lab of Los Angeles, CA — for printing the prints from the negatives.

J. H. Wright — who introduced me to first-day covers.

Collectors and dealers — who supported my first book, *Collecting Stamps for Pleasure and Profit*.

Federal Express — for carrying the manuscript.

The U.S. Postal Service (and its predecessor, the U.S. Post Office Department) — for making the stamps that I wrote about.

The staff of Betterway Publications, Inc. — for superb editing and book production of the raw manuscripts that I send to them.

ABOUT THE STAMPS ON THE FRONT COVER

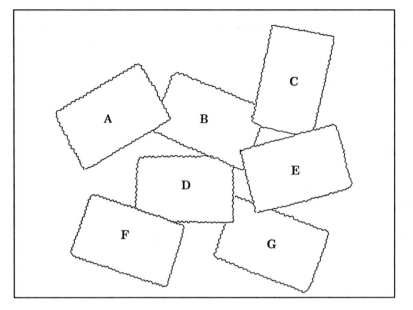

A. 48-star American Flag 4-cent commemorative issued on July 4, 1957. The first stamp to be printed on the Giori Press introduced in 1957 by the U.S. Bureau of Engraving and Printing to allow multi-colored intaglio (engraved) stamps to be printed in a single press run.

B. Boy Scouts of America 3-cent commemorative (Rotary Press printing) of June 30, 1950. Issued to coincide with the Boy Scouts second National Jamboree, Valley Forge, PA.

C. Wildlife Conservation 3-cent commemorative (Giori Press printing) showing adult and juvenile Whooping Cranes, a bird species that hovers near extinction in the central U.S. Issue date Nov. 22, 1957.

D. International Geophysical Year 3-cent U.S. commemorative issue (Giori Press printing) of May 31, 1958. This stamp called attention to the worldwide cooperaive scientific studies of the Earth and space during 1957-58. The hands and solar disc in the design were adapted from Michelangelo's "Creation of Adam".

E. Yorktown 2-cent bi-colored commemorative (Flat Plate printing) of Oct. 19, 1931, issued for the 150th anniversary of the surrender of Cornwallis at Yorktown during the American Revolution. Picturing Colonial Patriots Rochambeau, Washington. and deGrasse.

F. 15-cent U.S. Air Mail stamp (Rotary Press printing) of Aug. 20, 1947, portraying the New York City skyline, Statue of Liberty, and a Lockheed Constellation 4-engine propeller transport airplane.

G. Mothers of America issue of May 2, 1934 in honor of Mother's Day. Adapted from American painter James Whistler's portrait of his mother, entitled "Arrangement in Grey and Black." Printed by both Rotary Press and Flat Plate; also issued as Flat Plate imperforated.

Contents

Introduction 9

1 Starting in Stamps.. 11

2 Where to Find Stamps.. 19

3 Stamp Categories.. 29

4 Covers and Cancels.. 41

5 Handling Stamps 53

6 U.S. Stamps 61

7 Rare U.S. Stamps.. 71

8 Foreign Stamps.. 79

9 Defects and Damage.. 89

10 Errors 97

11 Investing in Stamps.. 105

12 Other Uses of Stamps 121

13 The Future of Stamp Collecting.. 125

Bibliography.. 131

Glossary 135

Index 147

Introduction

STAMP COLLECTING! A hobby without limits, a child's amusing pastime, an adult's leisure-time obsession, a scholar's fertile field of historical research, a dealer's source of income.

POSTAGE STAMPS! Carriers of a nation's correspondence, fragile specks of valuable paper, miniature propaganda posters of government bureaus, exquisite artworks of painters and engravers; more precious than gold, more delicate than glass, more enduring than fame.

PHILATELY! Searching the bottomless depths of a flat envelope, reconstructing the forgotten human beings who once made and used the stamps now resting in our hands, spending years and investing fortunes in the intellectual pursuit of elusive printing varieties, uncovering previously unnoticed rarities, discovering the wonder of paper treasures:

Gold Rush letters penned by lonely miners, air mail flown over the seas by Zeppelins, Prisoner-of-War envelopes (their contents long since censored), picture post cards sent by distant friends, Expedition Covers stuffed in the baggage of daring polar explorers — these are the things that stamp collectors know and love.

My first book, *Collecting Stamps for Pleasure and Profit*, has been well received by collectors and dealers, so here is another volume with a lot of material that I left out of the first!

Chapter 1

Starting in Stamps

And why not stamps? There are some for every budget, from 2-cent foreign pictorials to $200,000 Hawaiian and Mauritius rarities. You can collect mint, used, cancellations, on cover (envelope-affixed), off cover, singles, blocks, local items, foreign, regular issues, air mails, commemoratives, topicals (stamps with one theme like sports or animals), errors — in short, something for everyone!

This chapter offers advice and inspiration for you to *get started* in stamps. The costs, where to find information, stamp clubs, collections for beginners, and the reasons for collecting are all covered in this chapter.

WHY WE COLLECT   *Why do people collect stamps?*

For fun, profit, knowledge, and a chance to travel and meet new friends at stamp conventions and exhibitions. Curiosity about a geographical area of the world or about a time in history leads some collectors to specialize in certain stamps that reflect these interests. Winning awards in competitive stamp exhibitions, learning about other cultures, and the excitement of finding rare and unusual stamps bring joy to the hearts of true philatelists.

On another level, collecting anything is mentally satisfying because it gives us a sense of control and order in a complex and unpredictable world. We may not be able to solve the problems of Lebanon and Poland, but we can arrange Lebanese air mail stamps (over 800 different varieties!) in neat rows in our albums, and study Polish heroes in the Polish commemoratives honoring Warsaw citizens of past centuries.

THE COST   *What does it cost to be a stamp collector?*

You can collect for free by clipping clean cancelled copies off your incoming mail; $15 or $20 per year will buy most of the major commemoratives issued at the post office; and you can spend hundreds or thousands of dollars a year if you get serious about rare issues and postal history. There are thousands of stamps that you can buy for a nickel each. Ask any stamp dealer to show you some. Of course, many stamps sell for much more money.

THE CHASE   *What happens when I can't find stamps that I want? It doesn't look nice if there are blank spaces on my stamp album pages.*

The part of your collection you have already acquired is of minor concern. One of the beauties of philately is the thrill of the chase, the challenge of the hunt, as well as the pride of possession. If everything was easy to find, what would be the incentive? It is strange how the most desired stamps are not the ones in our collections, but the ones that we still seek.

U.S. COLLECTORS   *How many stamp collectors are there in the United States?*

That depends on what you call a stamp collector. The U.S. Postal Service claims that ten million or more Americans dabble in stamp collecting from time to time. But this figure includes the people who merely buy a new pane (sheet) of stamps from the local post office once a month, and tuck it away in a desk drawer to satisfy a hoarding instinct or in the mistaken notion that they will someday get rich when they sell these stamps which have a press run in the millions per issue.

The combined circulation of the most important weekly philatelic publications ranges from 100,000 to 150,000. The largest stamp collector's organization in the United States, the American Philatelic Society, has a membership of a little over 50,000. And the largest stamp auction companies have individual mailing lists of perhaps 5,000 to 10,000 active bidders, with maybe less than a thousand of those having serious money to spend (over $1,000 per sale).

Many people look at stamps, but not all of them are dedicated philatelists.

MORE THAN MONEY

If I can't get rich from stamps, what's the point of wasting hours in collecting them?

Money is one reason to collect stamps, and it is surprising how the true collector who has taken the time to learn about stamps is the person most likely to make a profit when the collection is sold.

Even the most famous stamp collections had to start somewhere. Your drawer of cheaper mint singles or common first-day covers may be worth little cash, but these items tell a story of your brief collecting history, maybe of your travels and the dealers or other collectors you've met.

When you have a few extra hours to spend (not to waste), take your stamps out and look at them. They're miniature works of art, creations of the postal services of ambitious nations. They're paper historical objects of the 20th century. They're worth saving and studying for reasons that would be hard to understand by people who care only about the cash price of things.

How much are your clothes worth? How much are the postcards worth that you bought and sent to friends while you were traveling? How much is a photograph worth if it is of a place that you visited once in your life and will never return to again? Stamps have sentimental and emotional worth, as well as investment potential. I have stamps that I wouldn't sell for a thousand dollars, even though I got them for $100 each, because they have a special meaning to me of the time when I was younger and eager to acquire precious stamps for my early collection. I didn't buy them for money, I bought them for themselves.

MIXTURES

What can I hope to find in a "mixture" of stamps? I see mixtures of U.S. and foreign stamps advertised for sale. How many different varieties are in an average mixture, and could I possibly find something rare?

Your reward for sorting through a mixture will probably be fun and learning. I wouldn't expect to get rich, in spite of the fabulous claims of some dealers who sell mixtures.

Mixtures are usually sold by the pound, either on or off pieces of envelope paper on which they were cancelled, with the seller estimating how many stamps you get per pound. You can buy them by mail from ads in the stamp weeklies, or at many stamp shops. Mixtures come in single countries (only the U.S. or Canada, for example) or with stamps from around the world, mint or used, definitives or commemoratives, low values or high values.

The typical retail price for a mixture of common stamps on paper ("cancelled on piece") is $5 to $10 per pound. Buy a small sample mixture packet from a dealer as a test purchase. If you like what you get, then you can order a larger mixture. Expect duplicates and common stamps in cheap mixtures.

STAMP WEEKLIES

Where can I get good current information on the stamp market? Are there weekly publications in philately?

Linn's, *Stamp Collector*, and *Stamps* are the three most important (and most widely circulated) weekly stamp hobby periodicals in the United States. They are all excellent sources of information, and most dealers and serious collectors subscribe to all three. Send a dollar and your name and address to each publication and ask for a recent sample issue.

Linn's Stamp News, P.O. Box 29, Sidney, OH 45365. Subscription price $28 for one year, $49 for two years, $40 per year for foreign addresses.

Stamp Collector, P.O. Box 10, Albany, OR 97321. Subscription rate $23.94 for one year, $39.88 for two years, other countries add $20 per year for postage by surface mail.

Stamps, 85 Canisteo Street, Hornell, NY 14843. $22 per year in the U.S. or Canada, all other countries $44.

Foreign subscribers to any of these publications should send a bank draft or international money order payable in U.S. dollars.

STAMP BOOKS

Do public libraries have stamp books?

Every one that I've visited does. Usually listed under "383" filing numbers on the circulating shelves, the stamp books in the public library almost always include several sets of Scott catalogs, beginner's books on stamps, and a small selection of specialty books on areas such as stamp topicals, air mails, the history of the mail service, and stamp picture books.

Of course, any stamp collector worth his or her tongs should check out and read all the stamp books in the local public library.

Where else can I get stamp books?

Every stamp dealer can supply current and some out-of-print stamp books. Visit your local stamp shop and see what's available. Collecting stamps without reading philatelic books is like sailing a ship without navigational charts.

What about stamp columns in the newspapers?

Many of the larger circulation general daily newspapers publish a stamp collecting column once a week. Ask the editors which day of the week it appears, and if they don't have a stamp column, ask them to get one!

I have been writing the question-and-answer column "Your Stamps" which has appeared in the "You" section of the "View" section of Thursday's *Los Angeles Times* since 1982, if they have space in that issue to include my column. In fact, the *Times* buys one-time publishing rights to my column's material, and they have given me permission to reprint any of my *Times'* writings in this book, much of which is based on these columns.

BEGINNING COLLECTIONS

What are good collections for beginners?

Anything used is a good way to start (because cancelled stamps are usually cheaper than mint), common first-day covers at fifty cents each (or less!), birth year stamps (issues made during your birth year from all countries), single country collections, home-town cancels and covers, stamps clipped off incoming mail, post cards and postal cards, and general foreign collections. Adult beginners should start out slowly even though they may be able to afford expensive material. The knowledge gained from handling thousands of stamps can't be purchased with money.

STAMP CLUBS

How do I find a stamp club? Or should I start one?

Ask other stamp collectors or dealers if they know of one. Most local stamp shops know of the stamp clubs that meet in their area. Meetings are usually in the evening about twice a month. Although you can have fun and profit from any stamp club, you'll feel most comfortable with people in your age group or with similar collecting interests. If you go to a school or work in a large company, get permission to poll everybody there to see if there are enough collectors to start a stamp club.

A stamp club meeting should provide members with the chance to buy or sell and exchange duplicates. A guest speaker who shows and explains his specialty is a common attention getter at clubs. Always have a raffle drawing with stamps or accessories (tongs, hinges, etc.) as prizes donated by club members. Avoid excessive club business procedure; collectors care about stamps, not about motions and measures and meeting minutes or officers' reports.

If you are starting a club, elect a president, secretary, and treasurer. Keep dues low to encourage more members. Five to ten dollars per year are typical dues for local stamp clubs with minimal overhead expenses. Have something planned for every meeting, including inexpensive refreshments like cookies and juice. Get a permanent location for the club meetings so that people know where to go such as a rent-free conference room of a bank or school. Publicize the club with posters or mailings to potential members.

Don't get discouraged if every stamp club meeting isn't great. Every session of the U.S. Congress isn't great, so why should a hobby club be any different? And *pay attention* to the members' wants and needs; it is everybody's club, not just a docile group that the officers boss around.

COLLECTIONS NEVER FINISHED

I want to start a collection that can be completed for less than $200. What countries or topics do you suggest?

And what do you do with this collection when you finish it? Start another one? Stash it away for twenty years in hope of a big killing in profits? Sell it out of boredom or give it away as a present?

I have found that the greatest joy in stamp collecting is the thrill of the chase, the difficulty but possibility of finding elusive issues, and the unexpected excitement that only comes at the moment when you discover a rare stamp variety that others have overlooked!

Philatelic Society memberships provide many benefits including expertizing services, contact with other members, and informative journals. $10 to $20 per year are typical membership dues.

Pick any country and time bracket, for instance, Norway since World War II or Peruvian commemoratives of the last thirty years. A representative showing can be made of these two specialties for about $200 apiece, if you avoid the rare items like errors or essays. The best collection is the one that is never finished, the one that you dream of constantly, the one that pulls you into some dusty stamp shop in a strange town, the one that you can always picture but never quite touch, the one that keeps you going as a philatelic adventurer!

Chapter 2

Where to Find Stamps

The paper chase, as stamp collecting is sometimes called, begins at home and ends at the most remote outposts on the Earth (if it ends at all!). The most treasured stamps in our collection are always the ones that we still seek, the ones that elude our tongs' grasp, the ones that may turn up tomorrow in the most unexpected place. To a true stamp collector, the joy of possession is trivial compared to the limitless thrill of the chase.

This chapter explains how to deal with sources at the Postal Service, city stamp shops, auctions, stamp shows, classified ads, and stamp society sales circuits. Remember, though, on occasion some spectacular finds have been made at antique shops, swap meets, yard sales, and estate auctions — where the seller may have no idea of the value of stamps. I once bought a wonderful group of old German stamps for a few dollars at a gun show!

U.S. POSTAL SERVICE *My local post office doesn't get all of the latest commemoratives. Does the Postal Service sell these by mail?*

Yes. The Philatelic Sales Division sells by mail all current U.S. stamps and some that have already been withdrawn from sale at local post offices. Also, useful philatelic books like *The Postal Service Guide to U.S. Stamps* (328 pages in the 15th edition, $5) and small stamp collecting kits are listed in the bimonthly *Philatelic Catalog*, available free by sending your name and address to:

> United States Postal Service
> Philatelic Sales Division
> Washington, DC 20265

Stamps sold through the mail by the Sales Division are at face value, but they charge a postage and handling fee of fifty cents for the first 500 stamps, $1 for 501 to 1,500 stamps, etc., and registration for valuable shipments is extra and recommended.

My neighborhood postal clerk won't sell me plate blocks from stamp panes. What am I supposed to do, buy the whole sheet just to get a plate block?

Postal clerks aren't obliged to break up their stock of stamp panes to satisfy customer demand for plate blocks. By not bothering them all the time, and by courteously requesting a plate block or two of a new issue, you have a better chance of getting on the good side of harassed postal clerks. Some of them will even save the plate blocks for you if they aren't busy that day, and if they have these blocks left over from selling stamps from the panes.

STAMP SHOPS

What do stamp shops offer that I can't get elsewhere?

Stamp shops offer constant free advice on philately, a steady supply of cheap material that the dealer knows you want, a weekly or monthly "bid board" of inexpensive stamps for sale, a professional opinion on the quality of the latest stamp collecting supplies, and a source of instant cash whenever you want to sell only a few dollars worth of stamps (that big companies or mail order dealers can't deal with profitably).

Of course, you don't want to abuse the goodwill and experienced advice of a stamp shop proprietor. If you never buy anything and if a paying customer walks into the shop, expect the dealer to give the other person his attention. But I've found that if you buy or sell even a small amount of material, a stamp store dealer will offer a lot of advice and useful conversation. Repeat business, of course, is in everyone's best interest.

Find your nearest stamp dealer's shop in the telephone book Yellow Pages under "Stamps for Collectors." Call before visiting to verify the hours that the business is open.

STAMP AUCTIONS

Where can I buy stamps at auction?

Here are a few prestigious and honest stamp auction houses:

Robert A. Siegel Auction Galleries
160 East 56th Street
New York, NY 10022

Rasdale Stamp Company
36 South State Street
Chicago, IL 60603

Superior Stamp & Coin Company
9478 West Olympic Boulevard
Beverly Hills, CA 90212

Harmers of New York, Inc.
14 East 33rd Street
New York, NY 10016

Christie's Stamp Department
502 Park Avenue
New York, NY 10022

Earl P.L. Apfelbaum Inc.
2006 Walnut Street
Philadelphia, PA 19103

These companies have floor bidding in person as well as honoring written mail bids submitted by customers who cannot attend the auction. Write to them asking for the price of their next auction catalog (usually costing from $1 to $3 postpaid). Christie's specializes in rare and famous stamp collections of U.S. issues, and their catalogs typically cost the most, about $8 each.

Stamp auction catalogs are an education in themselves, and catalogs of famous sales often become collector's items and reference works for the information they contain.

For an excellent mail bid stamp company (no floor bidders) try:

Gold Medal Mail Sales
J & H Stolow
989 Avenue of the Americas
New York, NY 10018

Of course, I have no financial interest in any of these companies, and there are many other fine stamp auction firms in the United States, but the ones mentioned have a long history and/or a wealth of rare and unusual material in their popular auctions.

And stamp auctions aren't a game. If you are the successful high bidder on a lot number, you are legally required to pay for it. If you don't, your name might spread fast in the stamp business as someone who is unwilling to live up to his contracts.

BID BOARDS

How does a bid board work?

In old-fashioned stamp shops, the ones that still cater to collectors on a budget, you'll sometimes see a large part of one wall covered with stamps in little plastic holders or glassine envelopes. Next to each stamp is its catalog number, the owner's (consignor's) number, and possibly its catalog value. On this identification slip you'll find a series of blank spaces arranged in a vertical column for insertion of a customer's bids with the appropriate bidder's name or initials. It is like a "silent auction" at a charity fund-raising event — the last bidder gets the item when the time deadline for the auction runs out.

The beauty of stamp bid boards is that you can see exactly the amount of money that has already been bid for a stamp, so you can top the last bid at a slight advance. Bid boards are also a great way to dispose of your cheaper stamps, and they give your local stamp shop business that it might not otherwise have.

Here is what a bid board lot looks like:

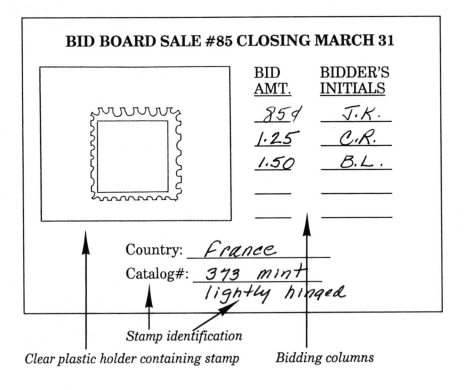

Clear plastic holder containing stamp   Bidding columns

Stamp identification

So after the store closes on the last day of the bid board sale, the owner of the store makes a record of the successful bidders, places the lots in envelopes with the winner's name and amount due on the front, and deducts his commission for running the bid board (perhaps 20% of the selling price per lot). The consignor of each lot gets paid when the successful bidders pay their bid board bills, although some shops with good cash flow may pay their consignors immediately as a gesture of goodwill and responsible business.

MAIL BID SALES

I see ads for stamp mail auctions, but I never bother to bid because I figure that the dealers only let their stamps go for bids near current retail prices. Is it worth my trouble to submit mail bids?

A mail auction (or mail bid sale) means that there are no floor bidders in person, i.e., the dealer picks the highest mail bid without having a public and open-room auction. The majority of all stamp auctions, mail and floor types, are honest and safe for mail bidding and will refund your money if the lot is misdescribed or not what you expected. Sometimes retail prices are inflated, or the dealer may not know current market values, or the dealer may merely want to get rid of certain material at any reasonable price, so feel free to bid low in any mail auction. All it costs is a postage stamp and your time to prepare and mail a letter. But consistently bidding very low may cause the dealer to drop your name from his mail sale list of customers. And many mail only auctions sell lots to the highest bid, not to a slight advance over the next highest bid as is customary with floor auctions.

RARE FINDS

Are there still "finds" of rare stamps being made?

Yes, but not as often as in the past. The reason rare stamps are valuable is that they are hard to find in the first place, and when they are discovered they are often in poor condition.

Get permission from family members to search through old correspondence and paper memorabilia (scrapbooks, old photographs, newspaper clippings, legal documents) and look for stamps and unusual postmarks (like war letters, censored covers, overseas mail). The fantasy of finding rare stamps in an old trunk in the attic comes true every once in a while for someone!

I've heard of a few sharp operators traveling around the country, offering to clean an old garage or attic for free if they can keep any stamps that they find. And believe it or not, people let them do this!

Long-established businesses may have old files that nobody looks at anymore. If you know an employee of such a firm, and can get official permission in writing to look at their files, you might uncover some interesting covers and stamps. It takes a bit of nerve and diplomacy to get into a company's sealed archives, but if you offer to split fifty-fifty anything you uncover, the company officers may let you look around. Have someone from the company present while you go through their documents, and don't touch files that they tell you are off limits.

STAMP SHOWS AND BOURSES

What are stamp shows and how do I take advantage of them?

A stamp show is held in a large room, usually a public exhibition hall or hotel ballroom, where dealers rent tables to buy and sell stamps in transactions with the general public. A stamp show also includes competitive stamp exhibits in which collectors display prominent specimens from their collections in the hopes of winning a prize or ribbon.

A stamp bourse is a gathering of dealers without the exhibits; in other words, just the dealers' tables. Although bourses are often called shows, technically a stamp show includes exhibits as well as the dealer booths.

Shows and bourses are organized by local stamp clubs, commercial organizations, and by national societies like the American Philatelic Society. Many shows are free. Those that charge admission typically have fees of fifty cents to $2.50 for adults. Often the U.S. Postal Service and the postal administrations of foreign countries have booths in which they offer their latest new issues at face value to interested buyers. Special show cancels and commemorative envelopes are usually for sale at stamp shows as souvenirs of the event.

The bigger shows have stamp society conferences (like meetings of the national War Cover Club or U.S. Philatelic Classics Society), lectures by stamp experts, and color slide presentations illustrating unusual stamps and covers. These meetings and talks are free to show visitors.

But the best part of a stamp show is the chance to talk to fellow stamp collectors and dealers who may have traveled from all over the country, and to see up close many unusual stamps in the exhibits and dealer stocks.

Dealers display their stamps under glass on their bourse tables, and they will be delighted to show you more items from albums and boxes behind their tables. Some show dealers specialize in expensive stamps, retailing for $50 each (and up). Others cater to the beginning collector on a tight budget. There are tables where you can buy classic 19th century U.S. covers for four-figure prices, and tables with first-day covers for twenty-five cents each, and grab bags or nickel boxes in which a dealer tosses all kinds of cheaper foreign stamps and sells them at five cents per stamp (your choice).

The great advantage of stamp shows is that you can shop around to buy or sell stamps by visiting dozens of dealers in a couple of hours at the same location. Don't be shy about courteous bargaining; some dealers deliberately overprice their merchandise at shows to allow for entertaining bargaining with customers. Standard terminology includes these phrases when talking with dealers at shows:

Is this price firm? (Translation: Can you give me a small discount?)

I'll pass on it. (I don't want it for this price or for another reason that I don't care to discuss, like the condition or maybe it looks fake.)

How long have you had it in stock? (Tell me more about it: Is it a popular stamp? Is it hard to sell?)

I'm just browsing at the moment. (I'm looking at the stuff that's out under glass on the tables, and I don't want to be pressured into buying anything due to a small spending budget today or for some other reason.)

Thanks for letting me look at it. (I'm a little embarrassed to have taken up your time without buying anything.)

When's your next show in this area? (I'm impressed by your stock and your fair prices, and I want to do more business with you soon.)

A constantly revised list of stamp shows coming up around the country appears in the philatelic weeklies (see Chapter 1), a vital reason to subscribe to them. And not all shows appear in each publication, so you've got to refer to all of them to keep up to date on shows.

Of course, dealers buy at shows, and don't be afraid to offer your material to a dozen dealers, rejecting all of their cash offers if you don't feel their buying prices are what you need for your stamps. Distress sales are always dangerous; when you desperately need money is the worst time to sell your stamps. And don't forget that auctions often bring the best price for top material.

So if you've never attended a stamp show, you're missing out on one of the joys of the philatelic hobby. Check the show directory in one of the stamp weeklies, and get over to see a stamp show!

CLASSIFIED AND DISPLAY ADS

How can I judge the validity of stamp ads in the philatelic press? I want to buy stamps by mail, but I'm afraid I'll get ripped off by crooked dealers.

Crooked dealers tend to get driven out of the stamp business because word gets around and they lose their advertising privileges and stamp society memberships.

First-time advertisers should always be suspect, and I wouldn't send a large order to one of them. The larger the display ad, the more low key it is (not promising the world), and the more often it runs in more than one stamp paper, the more likely it is that the company is stable, ethical, and reliable.

With classified ads you have to be extremely cautious. A one-time insertion of a small classified ad offering to pay big bucks for stamps, or to sell rare stamps at ridiculously low prices could be the work of a con artist. The stamp papers can't check the credentials of every classified ad buyer. Beware of post office boxes, of poor grammar in the ad, and of anything that says, "Act now. Don't delay. Send your money immediately before it is sold out!"

An honest classified ad might have this wording:

> 25 DIFFERENT U.S. PLATE BLOCKS AT DOUBLE FACE. IS-SUES BACK TO THE 1940S. $10 CHECK OR MONEY ORDER, INCLUDES SHIPPING AND INSURANCE. APS MEMBER. XYZ COMPANY, 123 MAIN ST., ANYTOWN, USA 12345.

To help guarantee that the ad is honest, clip the ad, keep it for a couple of months, then write to the company, enclosing a self-addressed postal card, and ask them if their offer is still good. Crooks usually hate to correspond, and post office boxes used for mail fraud rarely stay open long enough for the postal inspectors to catch the sharp operators.

I have an iron rule that I never send a lot of money or expensive stamps through the mail to any company that I haven't seen advertise for at least a year. Sure, every businessman has to start somewhere, but you have to protect yourself these days, and I'll send the little dealer a little of my business until I've seen his ads often.

If you place a classified ad to buy or sell stamps, expect anything from no responses to a flood of inquiries that you can't completely satisfy. So put the ad in only one issue to begin with, and see if you get any response before running it week after week. Use classified ads for cheaper transactions, display ads and local stamp shops and stamp shows for serious money.

SOCIETY SALES CIRCUITS

Can you explain how society sales circuits work?

Some of the larger stamp collector societies run sales circuits by mail. By placing your name and mailing address on their list, you can receive by mail periodic shipments of stamps or covers in your area of specialty, the material being owned and priced by members of the society. Payment for items kept is sent to the society which acts as a "middle man" between seller and buyer, usually at a commission to cover the cost of bookkeeping. Since only members in good standing can use the circuits to buy or sell stamps to fellow members, this is an incentive for collectors to be honest and follow the rules of the sales circuit department of the society. Anyone caught stealing from the circuit may be guilty of mail fraud, and is, of course, banned from the society.

The most famous circuit in the United States is the one operated by the American Philatelic Society:

APS Sales Division
P.O. Box 8000
State College, PA 16803

You have to be a member of the society to use the circuit which offers a wide range of material including eighteen different categories (like air mails, precancels, 20th century covers, plate blocks, etc.), individual countries and areas of the British Empire, Asia, Africa, both Eastern and Western Europe, Latin America, general worldwide, United Nations, and assorted topicals (like birds on stamps, music, space, or sports).

SELLING PERSONAL MAIL

Can I sell envelopes with stamps attached that have passed through the mails? And is there some liability or responsibility to the persons whose names appear on these envelopes, both the sender (return address) and receiver (addressee)?

When you mail a letter to someone, that letter becomes their property. They may do whatever they want with it, including sell it, unless there are special confidential circumstances involved, such as libelous or reputation-damaging information, or a court order or a written plea in the letter not to reveal its contents or to transfer ownership of the envelope or letter.

I recommend that you clip off the stamps on your incoming mail, leaving about half an inch of envelope paper around the stamp's borders:

Then save them in a box until you have enough to soak off or to sell wholesale to a dealer or to use as trading material or as gifts to other collectors. In other words, get rid of the addresses and names on the envelopes, and keep the stamps.

Chapter 3

Stamp Categories

A young child, ignorant of the many volumes which have been written on specialized aspects of philately, might glance at a box full of stamps and begin arranging them by color or size or shape or even whether or not they feel "sticky" (i.e., still have gum on the back). Indeed, the stamp hobby is so flexible and individualized that some grownups have been known to collect only blue stamps or only triangles (three-sided pyramid-shaped stamps) of the world.

Yet tradition and logic lead most of us sooner or later down the philatelic avenues of mint vs. cancelled, singles vs. blocks, definitives and commemoratives, air mails, special deliveries, postage dues, topicals, postal cards, souvenir sheets, overprints, charity seals, and assorted revenues like telegraph and playing card stamps. Like people and countries, stamps can be given classifications and categories which make them easier to explain and discuss. Let's explore these different types of stamps.

MINT AND UNUSED   *What is the difference between mint and unused?*

Mint means post office fresh gum on the stamp's back, as nice as the day it was issued except for normal aging over the years. A strict definition of mint implies that the stamp has no evidence of hinging or fingerprints on the gum. Never hinged (NH) gum must be all original and undisturbed by scuff marks or moisture smearing.

Most philatelists refer to "unused" as gum that has been disturbed in some way. The stamp was never cancelled and never saw postal duty, but the gum has been altered by hinging, handling, or storing. If a stamp has no gum at all it is still considered unused unless there is some evidence of a cancel present.

All this is important because discriminating collectors prefer original gum (OG), and will pay for it. A 19th century U.S.

stamp with original gum in pristine mint condition may be auctioned off for $2,000, while an unused version may bring $750 or less. Gum is often faked or repaired on expensive stamps, so if you don't know your stamps, know your stamp dealer!

CANCELLED (USED)

What is the difference between used and cancelled?

They're the same thing, referring to a stamp that has seen postal duty. Used stamps (except for undesirable cancelled-to-order junk from Third World countries) are quite collectible, but their prices tend to be less than their mint counterparts.

BLOCKS

Are blocks better than singles? Do stamps in blocks of four have more potential for future price appreciation?

Recent stamps (of the last fifty years) are worth about the same as singles or pro-rated blocks because so many have been issued and they were readily available when sold in the post offices.

This is not true of older stamps. Fewer stamp collectors existed in 1900 than today, and collecting blocks was expensive for the average person at that time. Many U.S. or foreign issues of ninety or more years ago are rare and more valuable in blocks of four than they are for four separate singles. Plate number blocks on the other hand are usually more expensive than the same stamp issues in regular blocks (with no marginal inscription attached).

Plate number blocks are especially expensive for mid-19th century U.S. stamps, and some are almost nonexistent. If you are going to save multiple copies of a stamp, get them in blocks, preferably with the plate number attached for maximum profit potential.

AIR MAILS

Are air mails good for postage in the United States?

Yes, all U.S. air mails ever issued are still valid for postage within the country and for overseas destinations. We no longer have a domestic air mail rate, but any U.S. air mail stamp can pay its face value for postage for the first class rate within the U.S. And any regular or commemorative U.S. stamp (except for a few that have been demonitized) can prepay air mail fees for overseas mail. (But don't use rare air mails stamps for postage.)

PLATE BLOCKS

Is it true that plate blocks can be collected in either blocks of four or six stamps? What is the best method?

Most U.S. engraved stamps since World War II are collected in plate blocks of four. The flat plate printing issues from the 1920s and 1930s are typically collected in plate number blocks of six, with two horizontal rows of three stamps each, and with the plate number visible in the attached margin paper over the top middle stamp or under the bottom middle stamp.

A glance at Scott's *U.S. Specialized Catalogue* will tell you how many stamps are customarily collected as a plate block for any given issue. As far as their value is concerned, most modern plate blocks (after 1940, with notable exceptions) are not that valuable anyway, but for the rarer plates you should collect blocks in the standard sizes listed in the catalogs.

COMMEMORATIVES AND DEFINITIVES

Which are better to collect, commemoratives or definitives?

Commemoratives are special event stamps honoring a person, places, or historical object (like a monument), and they are on sale at the post offices for a limited time, often a year or less. Definitives are also known as regular issues, are on sale indefinitely (often for five years or more), and are "small" in size compared to U.S. commemoratives. Definitives come in many different denominations, usually from 1 cent through $5 per stamp, while commemoratives usually have a face value corresponding to the current first class postage rate.

Both types of stamps have advantages and disadvantages: High value ($1 to $5 face) definitives and souvenir sheet commemoratives have proven to be better than average stamp investments over the years, but everybody knows that now, so recent issues tend to stagnate in market price because they are saved in large quantities in mint state.

In the last twenty years, the U.S. Postal Service has released over a thousand different major varieties of stamps, about 15 percent of those being definitives, the rest commemoratives. So there are more commemoratives than definitives to collect, but definitives tend to have more printing varieties (different papers, coils, booklets, plate numbers, etc.), so it can cost the same

*Souvenir sheet issued April 28, 1956 for the Fifth International Philatelic
Exhibition held in New York City. Sheet of two was valid as postage either
intact or as separate stamps cut out of the sheet. Produced under the authority of Arthur E. Summerfield, President Eisenhower's Postmaster General.*

*Canadian semi-postals, issued Jan. 7, 1976 to commemorate the 21st
Olympic Games held in Montreal during the summer of 1976. "Basketball,
Vaulting, and Soccer." The first denomination is the postage value, the
second is a surtax for the Canadian Olympic Committee. Retail $1.25 per set.
The United States has never issued a semi-postal stamp.*

*New Zealand Antarctic Expedition stamps in blocks of four. The 1911 Scott
Expedition issues are overprinted "VICTORIA LAND." The 1908 Shackleton
Expedition stamps bear the overprint "King Edward VII Land" in two lines of
type reading vertically; this block is cancelled with a circular handstamp
reading "BRIT ANTARCTIC EXPD. MR 4, 1909 (March 4, 1909). Unlisted
in American catalogs. Retail price $200 per block*

whichever you collect, but commemoratives tend to have expensive error varieties.

Which is better? They're both good. All stamps have historical value because they are the postal paper productions of world governments, and as such they reflect the politics, art, economics, and history of the issuing nation. I learned the names and locations of countries by studying my foreign stamps when I was a boy. Past and present rulers, flora and fauna, foreign currency and postal rates, and famous landmarks and buildings are a few of the things that can be learned from studying stamps. The value of stamps goes beyond money, and the person who sets aside a few hours a week to collect stamps will often be rewarded in ways that can't be anticipated.

SPECIAL DELIVERIES   *Are Special Delivery stamps still sold in post offices?*

Not in the United States. Authorized by Congress, Special Delivery service began on October 1, 1885, and since then exactly twenty-three major varieties of U.S. Special Delivery stamps have been issued, from ten cents (in 1885) to sixty cents (in 1971). The five 19th century U.S. Special Delivery stamps are scarce in mint condition, and their full-sized plate number blocks of eight or six stamps plus margin imprints and plate number catalog thousands of dollars each.

Special Delivery service was once quite popular in this country, and before 1970 actually got a letter delivered faster than the regular mails! Special Delivery covers are commonly found, and are an interesting postal history specialty, with routings and clock times often handstamped all over the envelopes. Bicycles, motorcycles, and fast feet were once the pride of Special Delivery messengers.

At present, any U.S. regular, commemorative, or meter stamps will pay for Special Delivery service, or what passes for such. And obsolete Special Delivery stamps may also be used, but only for Special Delivery fees.

POSTAGE DUES   *What are Postage Due stamps?*

These are adhesives which state the amount of money to be collected by a postal employee from the receiver of mail, because of insufficient postage affixed by the sender. Since the first series in 1879, 104 major varieties of U.S. Postage Dues have been released, according to the Scott catalog. Some early U.S. Dues are expensive in mint condition, selling for hundreds of dollars each when found with pristine gum. Postage Due stamps on covers are a relatively cheap and fascinating sideline to collect. At present, the U.S. Postal Service hand stamps and writes in pen the amount of postage due on a letter as often as they affix real Postage Due stamps to underpaid mail. Early 20th century foreign postage dues on covers are highly desirable.

TOPICALS

What are topicals?

Topical collecting means that you specialize in stamps that picture a certain theme, like animals, famous writers, trains, flowers, baseball, lighthouses, or topics that relate to a profession like medicine, law, art, teaching, or carpentry.

The beauty of topical collecting is that it can be less expensive than trying to complete a country's total list of commemoratives and definitives, for example. But topical collecting to its extreme can be costly, too: explorers on U.S. stamps might include the whole set issued to honor Columbus's voyages to the West. This 1893 set will cost several thousand dollars just for used copies in nice condition.

A disadvantage of topical collections is that they are sometimes looked down on by the judges at stamp exhibitions. And they are sometimes hard to sell, because not as many philatelists care about clock or cat pictures on stamps as are interested in air mails or general first-day covers. In England, topical stamp collecting is called "thematics."

Many inexpensive informative specialty books listing stamps of the world by topic are for sale by:

American Topical Association
P.O. Box 630
Johnstown, PA 15907.

POST CARDS VS. POSTAL CARDS

Explain the difference between post cards and postal cards.

Post cards have a picture on the back and are privately manufactured for the tourist trade. Deltiology, the study of picture post cards, is a hot field today, with cards showing famous people, war scenes, or controversial topics of eighty years ago in demand by collectors. Post cards are what you buy in the drug store or tourist stand when you travel and want to send someone a picture of your vacation spot.

Postal cards are blank on the back and are what you buy at the post office. Unlike post cards, postal cards have a pre-printed stamp on them, so all you have to do is write a message on the reverse side, address the front, and drop the postal card into a mail slot. Post offices don't sell post cards, so the next time you're there, say that you need ten postal cards and watch the clerk admire your philatelic vocabulary!

CHRISTMAS SEALS

Are Christmas seals of any value?

Christmas seals are not postage stamps, but pre-World War I varieties are worth a few dollars each. First issued by the American National Red Cross (1907-19), then by several National Tuberculosis Associations (1920-72), the current Christmas seals (since 1973) are sponsored by the American Lung Association, and all of them, of course, were sold to raise money for charity. Perforation and gum varieties abound in the Christmas seals, and most are cheap.

SEMI-POSTALS

What are semi-postals?

Semi-postal stamps are charity issues with two separate denominations printed as part of the stamp's design: the postage value and the charity value. The first number stated is the postage amount that the stamp is good for; the second number is the amount of money to be contributed to a specific charity, both values being the total cost of the stamp when bought at the post office.

For example, the popular Belgium semi-postals of 1928, issued to help finance the restoration of the ruins of Orval Abbey, have values like "25c + 5c" and "3F + 1F", meaning "25 centimes postage plus 5 centimes charity" and "3 francs postage plus 1 franc charity."

Austria issued its first semi-postals during World War I, and the "health" stamps of New Zealand are extremely popular semi-postals. Canada issued its first semi-postals in 1974, but the United States has never had a semi-postal stamp. While usually going to a good cause, the extra face value cost of semi-postals is sometimes resented by collectors who feel they are being tapped for money that they have to spend if they hope to have a complete collection of a country's stamps.

SOUVENIR SHEETS

What are souvenir sheets?

Souvenir sheets are special larger-format stamp issues made for stamp collectors and for promoting some event, usually an international stamp show (U.S. souvenir sheets), but sometimes just a way to get more money from collectors by the stamp-issuing governments.

The most valuable U.S. souvenir sheet is the White Plains sheet sold to commemorate the 150th anniversary of the Battle of White Plains, NY. First-day sale was October 18, 1926 at the International Philatelic Exhibition in New York City, and total printing was only slightly more than 107,000 copies, so it is a bit scarce today in pristine mint condition. With an original face value of fifty cents, the White Plains sheet now retails for several hundred dollars.

The later U.S. souvenir sheets are worth only $1 each or less, with the exception of the Bicentennial sheets of 1976 which retail for $20 for the set of four, and the special printings of the 1930s, which run about $20 per sheet.

SOUVENIR CARDS

What are souvenir cards?

Not to be confused with souvenir sheets (which are good for postage), souvenir cards are specially issued artistic cards, not valid for postage, but distributed to collectors at a moderate cost by the U.S. Postal Service or the Bureau of Engraving and Printing (for U.S. cards). These cards have major catalog status, and a near-complete collection of U.S. cards can be put together for a few dollars each, except for a dozen or so rarities which retail $10 to several hundred dollars each. Souvenir cards have dropped in market value in the past few years, so they seem to be a good buy at the moment, but not necessarily as a high-powered investment.

CANCELS

What kind of cancellation specialties are there?

First-day-of-issue cancels, machine cancels, town marks, bulls-eyes, hand cancels, flags and wavy line cancels, colored and fancy cancels, state cancels, pictorial and special events markings, and receiving cancels are a few cancellation specialties. It is thrilling to search through dealers' dime boxes of junk stamps in the hope of discovering a rare cancel that fits your cancellation collection!

REVENUES

Why are revenue stamps called "revenues"? Aren't all stamps revenues because they pay a government tax?

By custom, revenue stamps refer to issues that prepay a certain non-postal government tax, such as customs fees, hunting and fishing licenses, stock transfers, playing card and liquor taxes, tobacco taxes, and miscellaneous document taxes. U.S. revenue stamps date from the Civil War, and you might wonder why such beautiful old engraved stamps are so inexpensive today. The reason is that revenues are not as in demand by collectors as regularly issued postage stamps are. U.S. revenue stamps are often found badly off-center or damaged, and pen-cancelled copies are not as desirable as mint or handstamped examples. Only lack of heavy demand prevents U.S. revenue stamp prices from going through the roof.

"DUCK" STAMPS

What explains the rise in popularity of the "Duck" stamps?

The U.S. Hunting Permit Stamps (commonly known as the "Ducks") were first issued in 1934 for sticking on duck hunting licenses as a revenue-raising measure to help maintain waterfowl populations in the U.S. Through 1948 the Duck stamps had a face value of $1 each, but current ones, in the 1980s, are $7.50, $10, and $12.50.

Sportsmen, hunters, wildlife lovers, bird enthusiasts, revenue stamp collectors, and investors make up most of the heavy demand for Duck stamps in the philatelic market. Duck stamps from the 1930s will run you $100 to $500 each for choice mint copies, depending on the issue, and stamps from World War II on are much cheaper.

The Duck stamps look beautiful as a full or partial set framed on your wall (out of damaging sunlight, of course), and plate number blocks of the early issues can retail $1,000 or more each. Used Duck stamps are signed by the hunter and are quite cheap to buy — a way that a budget-limited collector can get a lot of the Duck issues without worrying about mint prices.

Future investment value? Probably good for the "Ducks," if purchased carefully now, with regard to nice condition and fair current market price (shop around a little). In the 1970s and especially in the 1980s, most state governments issued their own Duck stamps, which mimic the federal Duck issues, and which undoubtedly have been produced to cash in on the collector market.

GOVERNMENT SAVINGS STAMPS

What are the various savings stamps issued by the government?

U.S. Postal Savings stamps were issued from 1911 to 1966 to provide a method of savings for customers. The stamps were redeemable in the form of credits to the person's Postal Savings account, and were originally started to encourage savings from citizens who mistrusted banks, especially new immigrants or people in the Depression era who lost money in federal bank accounts.

With federally insured savings accounts at commercial banks and savings and loan associations, the need for Postal Savings withered away, and the system was abolished on March 28, 1966. As a little boy, I remember going to the post office in my hometown of Joliet, IL and seeing people buying Postal Savings stamps at a special lobby window. I didn't buy any for my youthful stamp collection because I thought they would never be valuable.

Plate number blocks of Postal Savings stamps are scarce from the early years. War Savings stamps (redeemable in bonds) and Treasury Savings stamps (redeemable in War stamps or Treasury Certificates) are rare and valuable in the dollar denominations. Both the War and Treasury stamps were issued by the U.S. Treasury Department, with issue dates ranging from 1917 through 1945.

TELEGRAPH STAMPS

When were telegraph stamps used? Are they rare today?

From the 1870s into the 1940s, many types of telegraph stamps were produced for various telegraph companies. Some varieties are quite rare, retailing for over $100 each, but most are quite a lot cheaper, many costing $1 or less. They can be collected unused, used on or off of the original telegrams, or with cut cancels. They are not government stamps, but were issued by private telegraph companies for use on their telegrams.

Western Union Telegraph Company was organized in 1856, and issued telegraph stamps from 1871 to 1946. Western Union, the telegraph company now operating in the United States, no longer attaches stamps to its telegrams. Telegrams themselves are usually not of much value, unless they are from a small company, have rare telegraph stamps attached, or have important contents of historical interest.

PLAYING CARD STAMPS

Why don't packs of playing cards have stamps on them like they used to?

Because the U.S. Internal Revenue Service playing card tax was repealed on June 22, 1965. People who bought playing cards in the United States before that date will remember the little blue tax stamp which was usually torn upon opening the top of the package's cardboard and cellophane wrapper. Most playing card tax stamps are cheap to buy, but some of the early surcharged ones retail for $50 to several hundred dollars each.

In 1862 the U.S. general issue revenues were first used for playing card taxes; the government tried to tax anything it could during the Civil War to help finance the war effort. Specific design playing card stamps were first issued in 1894 in the U.S.

LOCAL POSTS

What are locals?

Local stamps were issued by private companies in the 1840s and 1850s (with some continuing after the Civil War) to pay for independent mail routes, local address delivery, or express service. If you think the postal service is bad now, you should have seen it during the twenty years before the Civil War. Citizens relied on private express companies to deliver valuable packages (like gold or negotiable securities), and mail was normally kept in the post office (no delivery to street addresses) to await a visit by the addressee, not to mention the slow handling of mail by government Post Office Department couriers. The insistence by the government for a monopoly on mail transmission, by threat or actual act of lawsuit against the private local postal services, eventually drove them out of business.

Local stamps are the issues of these companies. Many are rare and valuable, many have been reprinted and counterfeited, and some have little or nothing known about them. Wells, Fargo Pony Express stamps are the most famous of the locals listed in the major stamp catalogs (and retail from about $40 to $200 each off cover), but many unpopular local stamps now sell for only a few cents each.

SURCHARGES AND OVERPRINTS

What is the difference between a surcharge and an overprint?

Both were added after the original printing of the stamp, but a surcharge is technically a new face value imprinted on the stamp, while an overprint is any other marking placed over the original design before the stamp is sold at the post offices. A loose definition of overprint would include surcharges, and you sometimes see this auction description: "surcharge overprinted double."

Surcharges and overprints are extensively counterfeited, and expensive copies of them should be bought with caution and with expertizing certificates. An example of an often-forged surcharge is the Vatican City set of 1934 in which the common 1929 stamps, retailing less than $50 for a mint set of six, is now worth over $1,000 for a pristine unhinged set with the surcharged values. The U.S. "Kansas" and "Nebraska" overprints of 1929 have been forged also. Any time that a cheap stamp is worth a lot of money when found with an overprint, expect that the cheaper varieties will have such overprints forged on them.

Chapter 4

Covers and Cancels

Covers! The real purpose of stamps — to convey the envelopes and cards that carry our written messages through the mail system. A "cover" is the stamp collecting term for an envelope or card that was designed to pass through the mails.

Like the human beings who made them, covers can be large or small, young or old, mysterious or simple, handsome or faulty. They range from common commercial covers, the envelopes retrieved from our daily mail delivery — interesting but probably worthless in monetary terms — to the rare and exquisite philatelic gems like Pony Express covers bearing Wells, Fargo locals of 1861 or personal free-franked covers hand-addressed by American Presidents while in the White House.

First-day covers, military covers, advertising envelopes, balloon mail, space covers (ones that have been to the Moon sell for four figure prices!), colored cancels, and stampless letters are each described in this chapter.

What is a cover?

A cover is an envelope or card designed for postal use. It may or may not have stamps attached (stamped versus stampless). It may or may not have actually passed through the mails (postally used vs. unused or "handed back" in the case of unaddressed first-day covers). When you're saving the whole envelope and not just the stamps, you're a cover collector.

KINDS OF COVERS   *What kinds of covers are there?*

There are many, which I'll discuss in this chapter. But basically there are two types or categories of covers: commercial covers, those which were routinely prepared by businesses or private citizens for ordinary mail use, without regard to any philatelic purpose; and philatelic covers, those which were specifically

A World War I British picture post card illustrating a soldier on the battle-field with a photo from someone back home, and the poem, God Guard You" at the bottom. Printed in England by Samforth & Co., Ltd., this card was unused. World War I post cards were more romantic and religious than World War II Designs.

1963 Scottish East Greenland Expedition cover signed by expedition crew. Mailed to the Royal College of Science in Glasgow. Explorer's mail is a popular branch of postal history.

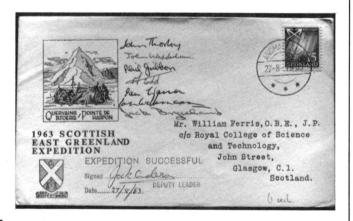

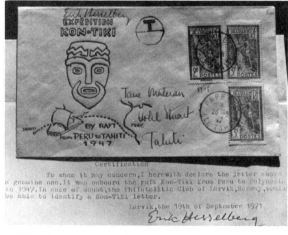

French Polynesian stamps on the Expedition cover with the certificate: "To whom it may concern, I herewith declare the letter above a genuine one. It was on board the raft Kon-Tiki from Peru to Polynesia in 1947. In case of doubt, the Philatelic Club of Larvik, Norway would be able to identify a Kon-Tiki letter." Signed by Erik Hesselberg, Navigator on the raft Kon-Tiki. Most of these envelopes were stored in a shoe box in the Kon-Tiki Museum in Oslo, Norway. The accompanying documents state that "Somehow, these letters were almost forgotten. The raftsmen very seldom met and so 23 years past (sic) until finally the letters were divided between the raftsmens still alive." The author has seen two of these covers and this is one of them, purchased by him at auction in the 1970s for about $150.

prepared by or for stamp collectors. Rare stamps in unusual combinations (like full sets or "mixed frankings" of many different issues) may only exist on philatelic covers, but commercial covers tend to bring the best prices because they happened by chance, and therefore show the true unplanned habits of users of the mail system.

GOLD RUSH MAIL   *I have an old Wells, Fargo envelope with an embossed 3-cent stamp cancelled at Placerville, CA. This cover is addressed to someone in "Mok Hill" and is in fine condition. Is it valuable?*

This is an early California cover, possibly dating from the Gold Rush years between 1850 and 1860. "Mok Hill" was a common abbreviation for the mining town of Mokelumne Hill.

Generally, these covers have no date in the cancellation, so look inside for a letter or document that might suggest the date the envelope was mailed. Gold Rush covers range in price from $25 to $1,000 or more each depending on: the stamp, the cover's condition, any mining letter enclosed, the route carried, rare cancellations, whether it is express company related, and the date of use.

For example, the cover you described from Placerville (formerly called "Hangtown" because of all the executions that took place there) is probably worth between $25 and $75 retail. If it had a miner's letter enclosed, triple its price. If the cover had a hand-drawn mining scene on the front, make it $1,000 in choice condition. If the cover was of the earliest known date from Placerville, add a few hundred dollars. And if it traveled by Pony Express (which it probably wouldn't have, being a local mining district cover and considering the date of use), add another thousand or so.

MILITARY MAIL   *What are military covers worth?*

Military mail, to or from soldiers in the field, as well as patriotic and intra-national (within one country) civilian censored covers, is a popular philatelic specialty. Prices range wildly, however, and you shouldn't be impressed pricewise by a cover just because it was written by a soldier during battle. Many letters are written during times of war!

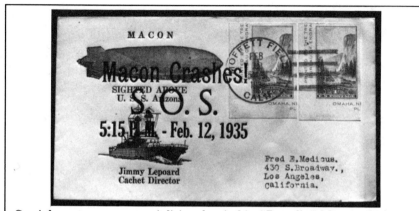

Special events cover memorializing the airship ("Zeppelin") Macon which crashed in a storm over the Pacific Ocean off California. Cancelled at Moffett Field, CA on Feb. 12, 1935, the black overprint announcing the crash was obviously added after the cover was prepared because the cachet designer couldn't have known about the disaster in advance! Notice the cachet notation "Sighted Above the U.S.S. Arizona," referring to the battleship that was later sunk at Pearl Harbor.

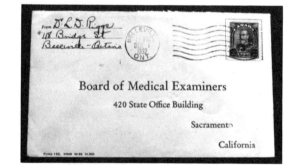

An immaculate surcharged cover from Belleville, Ontario, Canada to Sacramento, CA in 1932. Issued June 21, 1934, the 3-cent revalued 2-cent King George V stamp of 1930 is neatly tied on this cover. Pre-printed government reply envelope from California.

First flight cover for Helicopter service in the Chicago area, cancelled Joliet, IL, Nov. 21, 1949 at 11:30 A.M., backstamped received at Chicago Air Field, Nov. 21, 1:00 P.M. To St. Paul, MN. 6-cent stamp paid the air mail rate at that time. The U.S. has no current air mail rate for within the country.

Here are some typical retail prices that you might expect for certain categories of military covers (all priced per cover):

RETAIL PRICES FOR MILITARY COVERS IN VERY FINE CONDITION

Type of Cover	Time Period When Used	Price
Patriotic Design	Civil War: 1861-65	$25 - $100
Patriotic Design	World War II (U.S. involvement): 1941-45	$1 - $30, with most less than $5 each
Prisoner-of-War	Civil War: 1861-65	$75 - $150
Prisoner-of-War (POW)	World War II: 1941-45	$10 - $75
Censored with Hand stamps (including Red Cross and AEF mail)	World War I: 1914-18	$1 - $20
Censored with Tape	World War II: 1941-45	.50 - $5
Boer War covers, any country	Boer War: 1899-1902	$15 - $150, with most less than $50
Viet Nam War covers, any country	Viet Nam Conflict (U.S. involvement): 1964-74	$5 - $50, with better prices for POW material

These prices are for the *usual* material, those items you are most likely to find at a good stamp bourse, *not* for extreme rarities or expensive stamp frankings, etc. I believe that I have quoted fair conservative retail prices; damaged covers of inferior quality sell for much less, if they can be sold at all.

BALLOON POSTS   *What is a French balloon cover?*

In September of 1870, during the Franco-Prussian War, an experiment began with flying mail out of Paris via hot air balloon. Paris was surrounded by the Prussians, and this balloon mail was one way that the besieged citizens could communicate with the outside world.

Covers carried as cargo on these balloon flights are often marked with pen and ink "Par Ballon Monte" and are quite popular with collectors of (1) early French postal history, (2) war mail, or (3) early air mail. Retail and auction prices these days for French balloon covers are $100 each for average scarcity (common flights, common stamps and postal markings) and fine-very fine paper condition.

First-day cover of the California Gold Centennial commemorative issued on the 100th anniversary of the discovery of gold in California: Jan. 24, 1948. Actually some gold had been found in California previous to Marshall's famous discovery, but like Columbus, he was the person we all remember. This cachet (envelope design) is a bit more scarce than the Artcraft or Artmaster covers for this stamp issue.

Rerouted cover sent by air mail special delivery from Oklahoma City to Barrington, IL, then to Kirkwood, MO. It traveled pretty fast, having been posted in the morning (A.M.) of October 26, 1931, and being received at its final destination in Missouri at 10 P.M., Oct. 27 (the next day). Those were the days when special delivery was really special.

Imprinted corner card advertising embossed stamped envelope from the "Brooklyn Society for the Prevention of Cruelty to Children." Mailed to an address in the "City," meaning within the town of origin. 19th century social advertising and propaganda envelopes are popular among cover collectors. Pencil notation on the reverse side shows retail price paid: $35.

The French photographer Dagron originated the brilliant idea of microfilming messages which were attached to pigeons that had been flow out of Paris on the balloons. These pigeons were then released with their precious messages to be flown back to the place of their birth, Paris. Many of these messenger pigeons died during the winter of 1870-71 due to weather exposure, trained hawks, and German sniper fire. The "pigeon post" mail that they carried is sought after by philatelists, but genuine examples are rare and their authenticity is disputed.

WORLD WAR I CARDS

I have a post card from Vienna, Austria. The stamp on it is green, and the portrait is of the Emperor Franz Josef. The picture on the back of the card is a photograph of three army nurses. Does this have value?

Maybe $5 or $10 retail price. World War I picture post cards aren't as popular now as they were in the years immediately after that war, but there are still a number of specialists who collect and study them. Of greater value would be a battle scene, a bitter propaganda cartoon, or a photograph of a famous general in his World War I dress uniform (like Germany's Hindenburg or America's Pershing). Cards showing World War I military aircraft, biplanes and triplanes, are popular, as are any early airship (Zeppelin) views.

EXPEDITION COVERS

Can a specialized collection be put together of expedition covers?

Yes, at surprisingly reasonable cost. Submarine voyages, polar ice expeditions, jungle explorations, and raft trips have all been commemorated by mail carried by the actual explorers. Supply and demand determine the selling prices; $10 to $50 each are typical expedition cover prices.

FIRST-DAY COVERS

When was the first first-day cover issued?

The first officially prepared first-day cover in the modern sense is usually considered to be the one made by the old-time stamp publisher George Linn. It appeared on September 1, 1923, with a simple printed cachet in honor of the Warren G. Harding 2-cent memorial stamp issued that day. A cover like this in choice condition sold at a stamp auction in 1983 for $475, but since then I've seen them go for much less.

First-day covers of 19th century U.S. stamps are extremely high-priced, often thousands of dollars each, because they were not planned and very few have survived. Beware of faked and altered first-day cancels for expensive covers.

I want to make my own first-day covers. Where can I get the special envelopes?

High rag-content quality cacheted envelopes for first-day covers are sold serviced or unprepared, for those who prefer to stamp their own, by these two well-established companies:

> Artcraft Covers
> Washington Stamp Exchange
> Florham Park, NJ 07932

> Artmaster
> P.O. Box 7156
> Louisville, KY 40207

Write to them, enclosing a self-addressed stamped envelope, for their latest price lists of first-day cover envelopes. They sell the appropriate envelopes well in advance of new stamp issues, so that you have time to prepare your own covers by sending them to the official first-day processing city, etc.

SPECIAL CANCELS *How do I get a special cancel?*

If you mean one that is already in service somewhere in the United States, check the stamp weeklies (Chapter 1) for frequent listings of current special cancels and where to send for them. If you want to get a special cancel to be used at your local post office, there's a certain procedure.

According to the U.S. Postal Service Domestic Mail Manual, Section 170, a special slogan cancel request must be made to the postmaster at the post office where the cancel is to be used. The application must be submitted at least four months in advance and must include a description and date schedule of the event to be honored by the cancel; wording of the proposed cancel; name, address, and phone number of the sponsor who will be billed for the cost of manufacturing the die hub; and name of the post office where the cancel will be used. The postmaster will inform the sponsor of the approval or denial of the cancel request.

Medical advertising cover, U.S. Medicine Co., New York City. Cancelled March 3, 1900 with flag cancel (the stripes of which are the origin of our wavy line cancels), addressed to Pleasant Green, Phillips Co (County), Kan (Kansas). Backstamped with an indistinct town mark where it was received in Kansas in the "AM" (morning) of March 6, 1900. This cover, of course, traveled in the mail system by railroad train because the airplane was invented in 1903.

"Fire Marshal's Office. Joliet, Ill." government advertising cover from the author's hometown of Joliet, Illinois. Common 2-cent red of the time period tied on cover with a Jan. 2, 1899 flag cancel, sent to New York City. Hometown covers are a specialty of many philatelists.

Unused caricature cover of the Civil War, listed as #1177 in the Walcott Collection of Patriotics. Shows a white slave master trying to retrieve his black slaves, with the comments: "Come back here, you black rascal." to which a runaway slave replies: "Can't come back nohow, massa; Dis chile's CONTRABAN'" Retail value: $25 unused, $150 cancelled for pristine covers.

ADVERTISING COVERS

My old envelope has a picture of a shotgun on the left front side, and was cancelled in Connecticut. The stamp is a 2-cent Washington head. It is in nice condition. What is it worth?

About $20 and up, depending on condition and the rarity of the firearms company that used this envelope. You have what is known to philatelists as an advertising cover, common around the turn of the century and avidly sought today. Some gun companies like Winchester are still in business, and their 1900-era advertising envelopes typically sell for $50 or more.

"Nice condition" doesn't mean much in stamp collecting. Official, recognized terms to describe old covers are superb, extremely fine, very fine, fine, very good, and poor (in descending order of quality). Superb is the best, virtually as beautiful as the day it was mailed, pristine and rare! Poor is the worst, indicating severe paper damage such as large tears, pieces of the stamp missing, or large holes in the envelope. Few 19th century covers are superb due to normal paper aging, and very good or poor covers aren't usually worth collecting.

SPACE COVERS

I bought a few of the "Challenger" space shuttle covers that were carried on board on a flight before the tragic one in which it exploded. Can you evaluate these covers?

In the cargo bay of the Challenger were about a quarter of a million covers that were flown in 1983. Each cover should bear the $9.35 Express Mail stamp postmarked "Launched Aug. 30, 1983 Aboard Challenger" and "Returned to Earth Sept. 5, 1983, Edwards Air Force Base, California."

Originally sold for $15.35, these covers are now worth about $30 apiece. See the next question.

I have been buying space covers for each space shuttle flight. They cost $15 each. The covers are stamped with the dates of launch and landing. Are these a good investment?

The price sounds a little high to me. If they are not flown in the actual spacecraft, then they are merely "launch" and "recovery" special event space covers, collectible in their own right, but not scarce or as desirable as the envelopes that really went into space. Don't confuse these with the official U.S. Postal Service space shuttle-carried covers as described in the answer above.

If you could get each cover autographed by anybody connected with the flight, especially a member of the astronaut crew, the investment potential would increase. Chances are that the collectors who want these launch and recovery covers are already buying them as you are. If they all decide to sell their "investment," where will the buyers come from? Check the stamp weeklies (Chapter 1) for dates and where to send for upcoming space events covers at more reasonable prices than $15 each.

RARE CANCELS

Which cancels are rare?

Green cancels on mid-19th century stamps (beware of altered colors from the common blue); first-day cancels on pre-1900 stamps of any country (see the catalogs for the first day of issue); fancy cancels from popular towns like Waterbury, CT; hand-cut fancy cork cancels of the 19th century, like Ku Klux Klan, "kicking mules," and patriotic logos; earliest known date cancel for a 19th century town; earliest known use of a 19th century stamp (like Great Britain's Penny Black or the U.S. 1847 issues); the words "Prisoner of War" handstamped on a cover from a camp that had little mail service; "Pony Express" cancels on genuine covers of 1860-61; and foreign country cancels (especially Japan) on 19th century U.S. stamps.

Any of the above cancels can sell for three- or four-figure retail prices, but watch out for forgeries. A $500 cancel is tempting to forge onto a 5-cent stamp, so get it expertized before making a final purchase (see Chapter 13).

STAMPLESS COVERS

What are stampless covers?

Envelopes or letter sheets that passed through the mails without stamps. These covers might be: (1) free franks, the printed or actual signatures of politicians or other citizens who had the privilege of sending their mail free of charge; (2) 19th century letters carried by private courier outside the government postal system; (3) soldier's mail, which may or may not be delivered with postage due; (4) mail sent before the invention of postage stamps (1840 for Britain, 1847 for general U.S. issues) or before stamps became widely used (late 1850s in the U.S.). The last category (#4) is what most philatelists mean when they say "stampless cover," and these pre-stamp era U.S. covers run $1 to

$10 for common varieties, $100 or more for rare ones (see the *American Stampless Cover Catalog* by Sampson and Konwiser, the current 1986 edition for sale in two volumes, $50 each, from Leonard H. Hartmann, P.O. Box 36006, Louisville, KY 40233).

INAUGURAL COVERS   *What are Presidential inaugural covers worth?*

Since Herbert Hoover's term of office, inaugural covers have been philatelically prepared, showing an appropriate cachet design on the left front side, and the postmark of the President's date of inauguration. Some of the Franklin D. Roosevelt covers are worth $30 to $100 each. Eisenhower through Bush go for $3 to $10 each at retail, depending on the cachet.

The ultimate inaugural cover, of course, would be a handwritten personal letter ("autograph letter signed," or ALS in autograph business terminology) from a President, dated on his inauguration day, and mailed in a genuinely free-franked envelope on that day; the contents of the letter discussing his goals and fears in his new job! Such a cover would be auctioned for at least a few hundred dollars for an unpopular President, up to maybe $25,000 or more for someone like Lincoln or Jefferson.

Jefferson and Washington, by the way, wrote a tremendous number of letters in their own hand, and they are expensive to buy today because they are in heavy demand, not because they are impossible to find. And they both died long before stamps were invented, so if you find a stamp on their mail you know it is in some way faked.

Chapter 5

Handling Stamps

Countless stamps, rare and otherwise, have been harmed over the years because of improper handling. The fragile paper they are made of is so thin that 200 average stamps can be stacked on top of each other to make one inch. Even experienced philatelists have "paper accidents" in their stamp rooms, so the correct methods of handling and storing stamps must be continually practiced and perfected, such as:

Soaking stamps off covers; using stamp hinges, stamp tongs, magnifying glasses, glassine envelopes, and plastic holders; the various types of safes; and how to protect stamps in a desert or beach home — all are topics that get attention in this chapter.

Don't work on your collection when you're short of time: destructive flipping of album pages, bending a nice plate block, dropping stamps on the floor, and tearing the back of a stamp's paper fibers by overly vigorous hinge removal happen more often when you're impatient instead of relaxed and deliberate. Stamp collecting is not for the hysterical!

SOAKING STAMPS   *What is the best way to soak stamps off of their envelopes?*

Carefully tear the envelope around the stamp, leaving at least half an inch of envelope paper bordering the stamp's edges. Then immerse the stamped envelope corner in a bowl of cold tap water. After about ten or fifteen minutes, the stamp should float freely and can be removed with stamp tongs (blunt, rounded points) or with fingers.

It is best to soak stamps in cold water. Hot water may speed the process, but may also cause the ink to bleed off a stamp printed with what is called "fugitive ink," a type of ink that is water soluble. Also, an envelope that is colored like the kind used for birthday or greeting cards may soak its dye into the stamp and discolor it permanently if hot water is used (and often even with cold water). So soak the colored envelopes by themselves, by individual color, to reduce the chance of a colored envelope staining your whole batch of stamps.

Place the wet stamps face down on a paper towel (not face up, as they may still retain some of their gum and stick to the towel). Let them dry for a day, then carefully lift up each stamp with tongs and press it for a week or two under heavy books to remove curls and wrinkles. Be careful not to damage the perforations of a curled stamp when placing it under a book.

When should stamps not be soaked off of their envelopes?

When they are more valuable on cover, when it is a first-day cancel or other special cancel, or when the envelope carries with it an interesting history that would be damaged if the stamps were removed.

For example, the common 3-cent Washington of the Civil War era can be purchased from any dealer for fifty cents or $1, used and off cover (and without a rare cancel, of course). But when found genuinely cancelled on a patriotic cover of the 1860s, the stamp is worth from $10 up. And that same stamp on a prisoner-of-war cover can bring more than $100 at auction.

To be safe, leave a stamp on its envelope until you are sure you won't reduce its value by removing it. Any stamp dealer or knowledgeable collector can give you an opinion if you show them a particular stamp on its cover, but remember, once a stamp is soaked off, it may be difficult to replace it on its original envelope so that it looks as though it was never tampered with. Fussy collectors won't buy a cover if it looks suspicious in any way.

A general rule is that modern stamps from any country that you get on your everyday mail are safe to soak off (this doesn't include first-day covers, high value registereds, etc.). Old stamps, high denominations, and stamps with unusual cancels or interesting routing markings on the envelope are often worth more on cover than they are off.

STUCK SHEETS *I have dozens of sheets of U.S. commemorative stamps that are unused but have become stuck together. How can I separate these sheets without damaging the gum?*

You can't. Unless they're valuable issues, I recommend that you soak them apart in a tub of cold water, let them dry, and glue them on envelopes for postage or sell them to a dealer at a discount from face value.

Most collectors prefer original gum on their stamps. If your stamps have significant value as mint copies, you have a chance of saving part of the gum by using one of the humidifying boxes available from philatelic supply dealers. These boxes basically work on the principle that high water content of the air in a small enclosed box will loosen the gum of stamps stuck together.

STAMP TONGS   *May stamps be handled with fingers? If the stamps are cheap, what difference does it make, as long as they aren't damaged? After all, post office clerks sell stamps to collectors, and both of them handle the sheets with their hands at the time of the sale.*

Stamp tongs are time-proven devices for handling stamps safely. It is true that current post office stamps are cheap and can be touched with your hands. But remember, stamps are delicate objects, and their paper ages rapidly when exposed to sunlight, chemicals, high humidity, or heat.

Human skin contains oil, dirt, salt, and moisture, the same components that can damage a car's paint over many years. How much more fragile is a stamp! And it absorbs and retains the human skin chemicals which linger on the stamp long after you have touched it. If a stamp is important enough to save for five or ten years, handle it with tongs, for sale at any stamp shop for $3 to $10.

STAMP HINGES   *What are stamp hinges made of? Can they harm the stamp's paper?*

Good peelable hinges are made of glassine paper which looks something like light green-colored waxed paper without the wax. Hinges are gummed on one side, and come in flat or pre-folded versions.

If your stamp album pages are manufactured from good quality, acid-free stock, and if your hinges are glassine paper with safe gum, then you shouldn't do major damages to a stamp by lightly hinging it. The key word is *lightly*.

Glassine envelopes and inert plastic approval cards are convenient ways to sort and store stamps. The envelopes come in 12 standard sizes and cost a few cents each. Quality approval cards are 15 cents to 20 cents each.

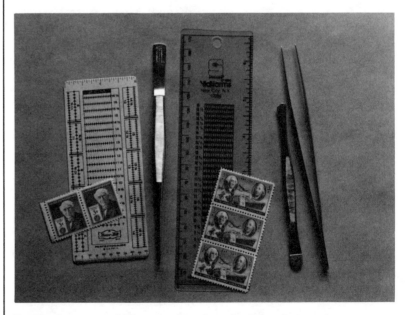

Perforation gauges (either metal or clear plastic) and stamp tongs are absolutely essential tools in stamp collecting. Gauges cost a couple dollars and tongs are $3 up.

Use just a little moisture (from a sponge or your tongue) to dampen a folded hinge, placing one half of the hinge on the upper rear portion of the stamp, then the other moistened hinge half on the album paper:

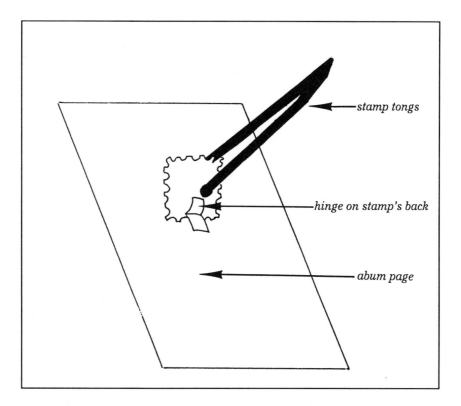

Rare mint stamps with original gum probably shouldn't be hinged because some collectors and investors frown on disturbed gum on quality mint stamps. Modern hinges produced today cause little if any damage to cancelled stamps when properly used, but some gum disturbance is inevitable when hinging a mint stamp.

Or to put it another way, European collectors of Vatican City, Austrian, German, and French stamps will often pay twice as much for the stamp if the gum is undisturbed, compared to the same stamp quality with the *slightest trace* of gum alteration from a previous hinge. Stamp auction companies are afraid to remove a hinge remnant from a rare stamp for fear of damaging it, exposing a hinge-concealed defect (like a thin spot or sealed tear), and angering the consignor.

MAGNIFIERS

What size of magnifying glass is good for stamp collecting? And how much would such a lens cost?

Five power (5X) or ten power (10X) are useful magnifications in philately. That means that these lenses magnify an object five or ten times its natural size.

More than ten power results in loss of printing details over a wide field of view, and shows the paper fibers as so large that you have a hard time discerning details of the stamp. A magnifier is used to examine postmarks and cancelling ink on stamps and covers, to help detect repairs and forgeries, and to discover minor varieties and printing mistakes. It is astonishing how much a stamp reveals when enlarged by a lens. Stamp dealers offer a selection of magnifiers ranging from $3 to $10 and up. My advice is to buy a cheap one at first; later on as an advanced philatelist you may want a ten power jeweler's loupe of quality optics costing $30 or so.

GERMS ON STAMPS

Are there germs on stamp gum? Is it safe to lick a stamp after someone else has handled it?

Studies that I have seen indicate no harmful effects from licking stamps for use on envelope mail. Bacteria and viruses are all over, not just on stamps, and those pathogenic germs that attack people are not especially fond of stamp gum as a food source. According to paranoid logic, we shouldn't eat food that people have touched because it might have germs on it. Or kiss babies or hug our pet dogs!

SAFES

Is a safe the best place to store stamps?

Maybe. It depends on the type of safe, and what happens to it during a disaster. A fireproof safe may release harmful chemicals or water inside to protect documents when its metal skin reaches a certain temperature; such safes have been known to damage permanently stamps stored inside them.

A burglar-proof safe might not be fireproof. A fireproof safe might not be waterproof. What kind of disaster are you expecting? How much are you willing to pay for a home safe? $1,000 will buy you a fair amount of protection, but professional burglars can get into any safe if they have the right tools and enough time.

The best safe for your most valuable stamps and covers is a safe deposit box in a bank vault. For about $20 to $30 per year, depending on the bank, you can rent the smallest box which is more than adequate for storing 3 x 5 approval cards or small glassine envelopes. Insure your stamps even though they are locked up, because items in safe deposit boxes aren't automatically insured by the bank.

GLASSINE AND PLASTIC HOLDERS

Some glassine envelopes that I've had for a dozen years have become brittle and slightly yellow-gray in color. Are these envelopes still safe for storing stamps?

I would replace them with new ones. The trouble with a lot of glassine envelopes is that they may have a sulphur content that tends to discolor stamps stored in them for long periods of time (ten years?). The Library of Congress has paper-preservation experts who suggest using envelopes or protective folders made of Mylar, a type of crystal-clear plastic that is apparently inert (harmless to things stored in contact with it). I have found that polyethylene bags and Plexiglas acrylic display holders are safe for stamps also. Local stamp dealers carry a variety of plastic mounts and sleeves and can recommend a type best suited to your needs.

BEACH AND DESERT AIR

I have a vacation home in the desert where I like to work on my stamp collection during spare hours. One problem is that the dry air cracks the gum of mint stamps. What can I do to prevent this?

You have the opposite problem that a seacoast stamp collector has. Philatelists who live near large bodies of water worry about humidity, mildew, and "curling" of mint stamps due to absorption of moisture into the gum and stamp paper. A desiccant chemical like silica gel available in photography stores should be placed around a collection kept in a humid climate.

In a dry environment, stamps may become brittle and their gum may crack. About 50% relative humidity seems right for stamp storage and moderate temperatures of 70 to 75 degrees Fahrenheit. If you think that excessive dryness is harming your stamps, try storing the collection near the bathroom or kitchen where water vapor is prevalent from time to time; in a small room with potted plants that you water frequently; in a room with open fish tanks; or in an airtight box. But be careful that you don't overdo it by making your stamps too moist and susceptible to mold.

Chapter 6

U.S. Stamps

Columbians, Trans-Mississippians, Presidentials, Parcel Posts, Olympics, Sanitary Fairs, tagged and untagged, Canal Zone, and United Nations — these are some of the U.S. stamp specialties discussed in this chapter. Air mails, the National Parks, and early 20th century commemorative sets like the Pan-Americans are forever popular among stamp collectors.

The United States has as rich a story in its stamps as it has in its history. In fact, U.S. historical events and people are specifically honored over and over again in the close to 1 1/2 centuries of U.S. stamp production (first general issue U.S. stamps: 1847). There is actually something for every budget, even in the sets and series which are often regarded as high-priced blue chip items.

You can buy the first two mint Columbians (1-cent and 2-cent values) for $10 apiece, lightly hinged, reasonably well centered. Or a fifty-year-old U.S. air mail in flawless mint unhinged condition for less than the price of a cup of coffee (the 6-cent Eagle of 1938, retail twenty-five cents). Of course, there are the more costly stamps like the 1930 Graf Zeppelins for $2,000 and up per set.

POPULAR U.S. SETS   *What are the most popular sets of U.S. stamps?*

Any list of the most popular would include:

Columbians   (1) Columbians. Issued in 1893 to commemorate the World's Columbian Exposition held in Chicago during that year, this set of sixteen denominations, 1-cent through $5, is forever in demand when found well centered and without damage. The 1-cent through 10-cent values should be collected mint, and the 15-cent through the dollar values either mint or cancelled. Notoriously off-center, the Columbians are a joy to behold when

Well-centered precancelled 3-cent "Victory" commemorative, issued March 3, 1919 to celebrate the Allied Victory in World War I Retail value _per_ _stamp_: $8 mint, $2.50 used; $100 for a plate block of six, $500 for a first-day cover. Well-known for its different shades of violet. Almost 100 million printed. Common on commercial covers, worth $2 to $10 each.

Precancels on 5-cent Postage Due of 1917 (Unwatermarked, perforated 11), 20-cent definitive ("Golden Gate") of 1923, and 9-cent Franklin of 1917. Precancels are known from the Civil War era, and they have been placed on stamps before affixing to envelopes to speed up the process of handling the mail. Precancellations are often worth less than a regular cancel, but some precancels are rare and valuable.

10-cent Special Handling plate number margin block of six, issued June 2, 1928. Used on fourth-class mail to secure first-class handling. Retail value _per_ _stamp_: $1 mint, 75 cents used. $15 to $20 for a plate block of six, $30 for a first-day cover. Part of a set of four denominations, 10 cents to 25 cents.

assembled as a set with wide, even margins. Get them with light cancels or original gum in the case of mint. Expect light hinging marks, and *don't overpay* for what is proclaimed to be unhinged gum. A dealer who has handled rare U.S. stamps for years recently told me that he has never seen a $3 Columbian with perfect pristine gum that he can honestly state is original unhinged.

Trans-Mississippians

(2) Trans-Mississippians. A shorter set (nine values, 1-cent through $2), the Trans-Mississippi commemoratives honored the Exposition held in Omaha during the summer and early autumn of 1898. Classic American scenes such as the "Indian Hunting Buffalo" (4-cent orange) or "Western Mining Prospector" (50-cent green) adorn the vignettes of the Trans-Mississippians. They all look beautiful in mint condition, especially plate blocks if you can afford them, and the high values (50-cents, $1, and $2) are a real challenge to find with large margins, light cancels, and no defects.

Pan-Americans

(3) Pan-Americans. Sold in U.S. post offices from May 1 through October 31, 1901, these stamps commemorate the Pan-American Exposition held at Buffalo, New York during that time span. Some of the public's criticism of the expensive-to-buy Columbians and Trans-Mississippians must have had an effect because the Pan-American set has only six values, 1-cent through 10-cent. The 2-cent railroad train stamp saw heavy use on mail, and over 200 million copies were printed.

There are so many different ways to collect the Pan-American set: mint ($500 total will buy a reasonably handsome set); cancelled, on cover, with Exposition Station Cancels; in plate strips and blocks; by shades; and errors. The spectacular invert errors of the 1-cent, 2-cent, and 4-cent values sell for thousands of dollars each, even when damaged.

National Parks

(4) National Parks. Issued on different dates during 1934 ("National Parks Year"), the National Parks set is often overlooked by classic collectors who hunger for great rarities or endless printing varieties. The imperforate pairs of this set sell for hundreds of dollars each. The basic set of ten stamps, 1-cent Yosemite through 10-cent Great Smoky Mountains, sells for less than $10 mint, but add the plate blocks of six (due to the

flat plate printing), matched sets of first-day covers, the imperforate special printings, and full panes of each, and you have a busy specialty. The National Parks are beautiful stamps, a set that a collector on a small budget can attack with the hope of acquiring something that looks presentable on an album page. Not to be confused, of course, with the "investment" value of the previously mentioned sets (Columbians, Trans-Mississippians, and Pan-Americans).

Presidentials

(5) Presidentials. Or "Prexies" in stamp collector slang. Issued on the eve of World War II in 1938 as a new definitive set of thirty-two denominations, 1/2-cent through $5, the Presidentials were for many years thought too common to merit serious study. Only recently has keen interest in commercial covers showing unusual Presidential stamp combinations arisen in the philatelic community. A framed set of Presidential plate blocks costing $500 or so looks impressive on the wall (kept out of sunlight, naturally!). There are expensive printing varieties such as imperforate pairs ($100 each and up) and the Internal Revenue watermark error on the $1 stamp ($250 each, mint). While literally billions of copies of some of the Presidentials were sold in post offices, every U.S. collector needs this set to complete the mid-20th century section of an album, and over the years the Presidentials have held their value (although increasing slowly).

Air Mails

(6) Air Mails. A complete run of the first 100 U.S. air mail stamps, issued from 1918 to 1980 in superb unhinged mint condition would take patience and money to assemble. Plate blocks, Zeppelins on or off cover, and first-day covers of the three 1918 issues will require deep digging in your wallet. The famous 24-cent inverted Jenny air mail stamp is in this set: selling price today about $100,000 per copy.

PARCEL POSTS

What were the parcel posts?

In 1913 a set of twelve carmine rose stamps were released by the U.S. Post Office Department (forerunner of the present Postal Service). They were designed to prepay parcel post (4th class) fees, and ranged in face value from 1-cent to $1. This set was immediately disliked by postal clerks, but contrary to myth, the reason wasn't only that they got confused because all the parcel post stamps were one color.

Henry M. Gobie, in his authoritative book, *U.S. Parcel Post: A Postal History* (1979), states that besides color confusion, postal clerks didn't want to handle extra stock or keep accounts with the unusual format of the parcel post stamps: forty-five per pane instead of the normal fifty or 100. Also, Gobie points out that the stamps were too big to squeeze on a small parcel in combinations.

The parcel post stamps were later discontinued, and they exist in collectible quantities on mailing tags, pieces of packaging paper, and on envelopes. Parcel post stamps were allowed to be used as regular stamps effective July 1, 1913, and they remained in post office stocks for a few years. Covers exist with parcel post usage into the 1920s.

Plate blocks, covers with the higher denominations, full panes, and first-day covers of any denomination are all prime parcel post stamp materials running in cost from three- to five-figure prices. Avoid straight edges and off-center copies.

DUCK STAMPS   *Why are the Duck Stamps so popular?*

According to Bob Dumaine, a Houston stamp dealer whose store I visited recently (and who is a recognized Duck Stamp specialist broker), the Hunting Permit Stamps (commonly known as the "Ducks") appeal to stamp collectors, sportsmen, bird lovers, and wildlife enthusiasts. The wide market appeal, the wide price range (something for every budget), and the beauty of the federal Duck stamps themselves assures their popularity.

First issued in 1934, the federal Hunting Permit Stamps come out every year. Revenues from their original purchase go to maintain U.S. waterfowl life. The first Duck stamp in 1934 had a face value of $1. Current stamps are $12.50 face value. On a tight collecting budget you can buy them used, meaning signed across the stamp's face by the hunter. A bit more money will secure fine, mint, lightly hinged copies.

But the serious Duck Stamp funds go into full plate blocks, mint superb unhinged singles, and rare varieties like imperforate pairs. Many state governments have issued their own "Duck" revenue stamps since the 1970s, and the "#1" issues of each state are prime investment items.

LOS ANGELES OLYMPICS STAMPS

I have a 1984 Los Angeles Olympics "Golden Moments" stamp album with postal cancellations of the venue of each Olympic event. I received this album as a gift and would like to know its value.

It is still a little early to fix a definitive price on 1984 Olympic material. As a visitor to the 1984 Los Angeles Olympics, I was overwhelmed by the avalanche of souvenirs, folders, pins, flags, coins, and stamps that were for sale all around the Los Angeles Coliseum. Most stamp-issuing countries flood the market with Olympic stamps every four years, and the 1984 Olympics brought a great amount of souvenirs from America because the Games were held here. I've seen the albums that you describe and I'd say they are worth $40 or $50 retail today.

You didn't by chance get Mary Decker's or Zola Bud's autograph in your album on the day of their race? Or Carl Lewis's dated signature on his photograph at the Games? The things that are most rare are *not* what everybody else has, but what only you have!

SPECIALIZED COLLECTING: THE 2-CENT COLUMBIAN

How can anyone specialize in a single stamp? What is there to know that could take up so much time and effort?

Consider the 2-cent Columbian commemorative of 1893 showing the "Landing of Columbus." Almost 1 1/2 *billion* copies were printed, making it a cheap source of endless cancelled specimens (five cents to twenty cents each). You can collect it by different types of cancel, arranging these cancels on album pages. You can collect it on cover showing first class, overweight, or foreign mail use. You can collect it mint, in strips, in singles ($10-$20), in blocks, and in plate number blocks. For $300 you can buy a mint off-center 2-cent Columbian plate block of eight!

You can get imperf pairs (for around $1,000), double transfers ($20 mint, twenty cents cancelled), and the "broken hat" printing varieties ($40 mint, twenty cents used). You can study its gum, you can study its paper, you can research its design. Expensive plate proofs on India paper and on cardboard are available (several hundred dollars each). You can search dealers' stockbooks for shades. You can track down printing oddities like misperfed, overinked, underinked, plate smears, and pre-printing paper folds.

$1 Hunting Permit Stamp of 1945, with the notation "Void After June 30, 1946." The 12th annual federal "Duck" stamp, sowing "Shoveller Ducks in Flight." Retail value $25 mint, $7.50 used, $175 for a plate block of six.

1-cent U.S. Parcel Post stamp: "Post Office Clerk," issued Jan. 1, 1913. Retail value $3 mint, 65 cents used, $80 for plate block of six, $650 for a first-day cover with July 1, 1913 date when Parcel Post stamps were legally usable on regular mail. Copy shown is just fine: perforations barely clear of the design. Over 200 million printed in 1913-14.

Private Die Proprietary stamps: John F. Henry "U.S. Medicine Warehouse, New York" and Dr. Williams Medicine Co. ("Pink Pills for Pale People"). Started as a revenue-raising measure during the Civil War, the proprietary medicine tax was levied on patent medicines at the rate of 1 cent for each 25 cents of retail price up to $1, then 2 cents for each 50 cents in excess of $1. Long neglected by the mainstream of philately, these stamps are becoming more popular and their prices are rising.

If you have the big bucks, you can buy at auction a first-day cover ($1,500 to $2,000) or complete panes of the 2-cent Columbian (several thousand dollars). Exposition station cancels ($100 and up), foreign mail usage, and combination covers with mixed franking U.S./foreign stamps can round out your specialty of this stamp. And when you're all done with this, you still won't know everything because you will have seen and handled only a tiny fraction of the 2-cent Columbians in existence!

People specialize in a single issue because they get obsessed with a stamp's design, its history, or the interesting varieties that it has. It's that simple!

SANITARY FAIRS

What were the Sanitary Fairs?

During the Civil War, a number of Sanitary Fairs were held to raise money for aiding the health of Union troops. Eight of these Fairs issued special stamps, not valid for postage, but still affixed and used on envelopes at Fair post offices.

The Great Central Fair at Philadelphia issued 10-cent, 20-cent, and 30-cent face value stamps, which are currently available from dealers for around $10 each. On cover with cancels of the time period the Sanitary Fair stamps cost hundreds of dollars; beware of forged cancels. And watch out for reprints and counterfeits of the stamps themselves.

STAMP PRINTING TOTALS

What is an average total printing run for a U.S. stamp?

In the billions for a definitive (regular issue) of low denomination that sees frequent postal duty. About 160 million for an average commemorative of the last twenty years. The two Christmas stamps issued each year have a combined press run of over one billion copies.

So you see, modern U.S. stamps with enormous press runs are a poor investment because the supply will always outpace the demand for them in our lifetimes. Collecting errors and scarce plate block numbers are ways to get around this problem.

DEMONITIZED STAMPS

Are all U.S. stamps ever issued still valid for postage use?

No. Unlike U.S. coins, all of which since the first regularly struck ones in 1793 are still legal tender, some U.S. stamps have been declared invalid for postage. When the Civil War broke out in 1861, the stamps available at post offices in 1860 were demonitized so that large stocks of stamps in Confederate states' post offices couldn't somehow be used to damage the North financially. Postmasters were given time to return the old stamps to the Post Office Department in Washington.

The 1847 first general issue U.S. stamps, the 5-cent Franklin and 10-cent Washington, were declared invalid for postal use as of July 1, 1851. So the rare and valuable pre-Civil War U.S. stamps today cannot legally be used as postage on mail, not that anyone would want to, because the first U.S. issues are, with few exceptions (like the 90-cent blue of 1860), worth much more unused than cancelled.

STAMP TAGGING (LUMINESCENCE)

Explain luminescent stamps.

Luminescent stamps glow with a different color when placed under an ultraviolet light. There are two basic kinds of luminescent stamps: fluorescent ones, which glow due to the fluorescent paper from which they are made; and phosphorescent ones that continue to glow a little while after the ultraviolet (UV) lamp is turned off.

Since 1963, many U.S. stamps have been *tagged,* or coated with a phosphorescent chemical that can be detected by automatic sorting and cancelling machines at mail processing centers. The philatelic study of "tagged" stamps is a lively specialty, requiring a UV lamp (costing $50 to $100, sold by the bigger stamp shops) and a catalog that lists which stamps are tagged. Production errors in the phosphor tagging are one of the things that collectors look for, such as untagged stamps that are supposed to be tagged.

And remember to avoid looking at the lamp's bulb when it is on so that you don't hurt your eyes with the intense UV rays. You can wear safety goggles just to be on the safe side; these goggles filter out the harmful UV rays.

CANAL ZONE

Are Canal Zone stamps still being produced?

No. The last formal Canal Zone issue was released in October 1978, during President Carter's administration. As you may remember, Carter negotiated a treaty with Panama, effectively giving the Panama Canal to Panama (subject to U.S. military needs). Under U.S. control from 1904 to 1979, the Canal Zone Postal Service stopped operating on September 30, 1979, and the country of Panama now handles mail there. Canal Zone stamps are classified as a former U.S. possession, and as such are collected as a U.S. philatelic sideline.

UNITED NATIONS

A few years ago, on the advice of a financial newsletter, I purchased some United Nations stamps for $400. Recently a dealer offered me $50 for the whole lot. They were to increase handsomely in value. What happened?

United Nations (U.N.) stamps have dropped in price during the stamp recession of the past decade, and maybe you overpaid to begin with. Consider yourself lucky — you *only* lost a few hundred dollars in the process of learning that stamps can decrease as well as increase in value. If the writer of that newsletter followed his own advice with his life savings, he probably went bankrupt.

On the other hand, U.N. stamps are popular among collectors and most issues can be obtained at very moderate cost. First sold in 1951, U.N. stamps have been collected by philatelists and used on mail posted by tourists and diplomats at the post office in the U.N. building in New York City. U.N. stamps may only be used at the appropriate U.N. postal facility in New York, Geneva, or Vienna (special stamps for these other cities).

An order form for purchasing stamps from the United Nations may be obtained by writing to:

United Nations Postal Administration
P.O. Box 5900
Grand Central Station
New York, NY 10017

And back issues (non-current) of United Nations stamps can be bought at your local stamp shop; most neighborhood stamp stores carry U.N. stamps in stock.

Chapter 7

Rare U.S. Stamps

Postage currency, revenue inverts, and high values, the 1-cent blue Z-Grill, $5 definitives, the ever-popular Graf Zeppelins, Confederate States Provisionals, encased postage stamps — these have got to be part of the list of minor to major U.S. philatelic rarities, as well as items like the Columbians and Trans-Mississippians discussed in Chapter 6.

"Rarity" is a relative term, rendered more ambiguous due to its overuse and abuse. Some stamps are rare but not valuable (*unpopular* locals or precancels). Some stamps are valuable but not rare (the first issues of the U.S. and Great Britain, the 5-cent Franklin and the 10-cent Washington, and the Penny Black). Some are rare (not in *every* auction) *and* valuable (Pony Express adhesives on cover, some Confederate Provisionals).

It also depends on the size of our wallet when we classify stamps as rare or common: If your stamp budget is $50 per month, then a $350 mint 65-cent Zeppelin may seem like an unobtainable rarity!

CIVIL WAR POSTAGE CURRENCY

I have some postage currency in the denominations of 5, 10, 25, and 50 cents. When I was a child, I was told that this type of currency was used for the Pony Express, and for this purpose was used as money to cover the cost of postage. Do these things have value today?

Due to the extreme shortage of coins during the Civil War because of bullion hoarding by nervous citizens, the U.S. Congress authorized the printing of paper money with the designs of the current postage stamps to be used as small change in daily commerce. Also known as "fractional currency" in coin collector talk, these items are often found badly creased, faded, or torn, making them worth not much more than face value.

Issued from 1862 and remaining in circulation until about 1876, these postage currency notes normally retail from $20 to $200 each when encountered in near uncirculated state, more for rare varieties like scarce signatures in crisp new condition. If your specimens are worn or dirty, they are worth at most only a few dollars each.

The origin of postage currency is interesting. People were actually circulating mint postage stamps during the Civil War when coins became uncommon, and the federal government decided to take advantage of the public's ready acceptance of U.S. stamps by issuing postage currency which resembled the stamps in appearance. Smaller than dollar bills of the time, this postage currency found acceptance as a change-making medium in stores, and was more convenient than carrying around stuck-together dirty stamps which were more fragile than the postal currency.

U.S. REVENUES

Are U.S. revenues rare? What is their price range?

The first issue of U.S. revenues appeared in the winter of 1862-63, during the Civil War. Many of these early revenues aren't rare today, retailing for only a few cents each, except for rare paper and perforation varieties. They were created to raise funds in the financially strapped North, and they paid taxes on official documents like bank checks or telegrams. The 1-cent red and 3-cent green Playing Card revenues of this time period are especially desirable in undamaged blocks of four, in which case they are worth several hundred dollars.

The second issue of U.S. revenues (1871) was caused by reports of fraud in cleaning and reusing the first issue stamps. The second issue had new designs and different paper having silk threads in it. Inverted centers, with George Washington's portrait upside down, are prime rarities in this second issue set; some of these inverts retail for $2,000 to $5,000 each. And the $200 and $500 values of the second issue revenues are also in high demand, priced at around $3,500 and $9,000 respectively for reasonably nice copies.

There are hundreds of U.S. revenues worth between $10 and $200 apiece, and many more, including varieties, retailing for $5 each or less. Old revenues are often ornately engraved, well-printed, and of great historical interest to stamp specialists. Because fewer collectors specialize in revenues than in commemoratives or definitives, you can pick up rare revenue issues for a fraction of the price they would be worth if they were a general postage stamp.

1-CENT Z-GRILL   *Why is the 1-cent blue Z-Grill so valuable?*

On November 10, 1986, Superior Stamp & Coin Company of Beverly Hills, CA auctioned off the 1-cent blue Z-Grill U.S. regular issue of 1867, often called the rarest U.S. stamp because this is the only copy available to collectors; the other specimen being locked up in the Miller Collection of the New York Public Library. Listed as Lot #186, this stamp showing Benjamin Franklin was knocked down for a bid of $380,000 plus a ten percent auction commission for a total of $418,000, the most expensive U.S. stamp ever auctioned up until that moment!

The "Z-Grill" refers to the scarce grill dimension of 11 x 14 millimeters, which appears on stamps of other denominations of the period, but is rare to the point of two known copies in the case of the 1-cent Franklin. This stamp is needed by sophisticated collectors to complete a set of 19th century U.S. stamps. In other words, it is rare and desirable and only one person at a time can ever hope to own it (unless, of course, you buy it as a partnership, as a group of investors actually did with the fabulous 1-cent British Guiana a few years ago).

Grills are little bumps or indentations that were impressed into the paper of certain U.S. 19th century stamps so that the canceling ink would penetrate the stamp's fibers and make it difficult to fraudulently remove the stamp's cancel for illegal reuse of the stamp. The Z-Grill is unique because it is horizontal instead of the normal vertical position relative to the stamp's design.

$5 DEFINITIVES   *Are the $5 regular issues a good investment? What is the difference in their desirability either from a philatelic or financial standpoint?*

Anytime the post office charges $5 for one stamp, you'll find that very few are sold compared with their much cheaper cousins. And the further you go back in time, the more money was worth, and the rarer are the $5 denomination stamps. When $5 was a decent wage for some people in the late 19th century (per *day*, not per hour), it was a serious chunk of money to lay out for a postage stamp either for actual postal use or more extravagantly for collecting purposes.

So the $5 denomination U.S. stamps are in general choice investment items over the long haul. The $5 black Columbian Exposition issue will set you back $3,000 or $4,000 for a lovely mint copy today; when it was first sold in post offices in 1893, the face value was $5. The $5 dark green John Marshalls of 1894-1903 retail for $1,500 to $2,500 apiece mint, while the more common but still popular $5 Head of Freedom Statue issue of 1923 in gorgeous carmine and blue colors can be purchased for a few hundred dollars mint; find it as a plate number block of eight and you're talking $4,500.

The $5 Coolidge of the classical Presidential series of 1938 now sells for about $85 mint, and the $5 Hamilton of 1956 retails at $70.

GRAF ZEPPELINS

Are the U.S. Graf Zeppelins valuable because they are rare or because they are popular?

A little of both, or maybe I should say a lot of the latter. The U.S. Postal Service gives statistics of press runs of between 61,000 and 94,000 for each of the three Graf Zeppelins, not an impossibly scarce quantity for a heavily-saved mid-20th century air mail issue, but demand is perennially high, therefore the current retail price of about $2,400 for a mint set of three, $1,200 for a nice used set, a bit more for pristine superb flawless copies.

The famous Graf Zeppelins were issued on April 19, 1930 for use on letters carried on the first flight of the German airship "Graf Zeppelin" between Europe and America. At the start of the Great Depression, most collectors couldn't afford to buy these expensive air mails which bore the denominations 65-cents (green), $1.30 (brown), and $2.60 (blue). So on June 30, 1930, the Graf Zeppelins were withdrawn from sale, assuring them a place in philatelic history and a pain in the wallet for budget-conscious collectors of later generations.

Beware of re-gummed, re-perforated, and sealed tears on these Zeppelin stamps; their great value invites unscrupulous repairs on damaged copies. It is legal to buy or sell damaged or repaired stamps as long as they aren't misrepresented as being flawless.

THE 1847 ISSUES

Why are the first two U.S. stamps so valuable? Every big auction seems to have a selection of them. It is because they were the first stamps?

Yes! Due to the mystique and romance of being the first general issue U.S. adhesive postage stamps, the 5-cent red brown Franklin and the 10-cent black Washington are forever popular among philatelists. For choice copies with wide margins and no flaws, the 5-cent value currently retails at $3,000 to $5,000 mint, $500 to $1,000 used. The 10-cent Washington goes for around $10,000 or more with full gum, $1,000 to $2,500 cancelled.

But condition is all important for these first imperforates, and stamps with surface scuffs, tiny thins, "sealed" tears, bleached-out pen cancels, heavy distracting "killer" cancels, or faked gum will sell at a steep discount from their undamaged cousins. Issued July 1, 1847, these two stamps are indeed in almost every large U.S. auction, yet choice copies always find ready buyers. They are especially nice in pairs, blocks, and on clean covers, but you had better have a deep wallet if you plan to specialize in these first issues: spectacular covers and blocks routinely auction off for five-figure hammer prices.

CONFEDERATE PROVISIONALS

How rare are the Confederate States Postmasters' Provisionals?

Some are unique, only one example being known of those varieties, and if they have any appreciable demand, are worth between $10,000 and $100,000 each at auction. During the summer and early fall of 1861, when U.S. government stamps were unavailable for use in the Confederacy, some local Confederate Postmasters issued their own Provisionals. Some of these are crude hand stamps, others are makeshift adhesives quickly prepared to meet the postal needs of a local populace.

Examples of unique and valuable Confederate Provisionals are the 5-cent red on amber Austin, Mississippi; the 10-cent rectangular black on yellow Beaumont, Texas; the 5-cent blue on buff Franklin, North Carolina; and the 5-cent red-brown on cover Mount Lebanon, Louisiana. If you are rich and want to own something precious and philatelically irreplaceable, buy some Confederate Postmasters' Provisionals, with expertizing certificates, of course, to help guarantee their authenticity!

A lovely pre-cancelled horizontal strip of three of the 2-cent Black Jack definitive of July, 1963 (earliest known use: July 6). This is the ungrilled variety. Superb copies of the Black Jack with large margins and no defects are almost nonexistent; what auction catalogs call superb are really very fine to extremely fine Black Jacks which are normally notoriously off-center. The author paid $90 for this strip at auction in the 1970s.

Two horizontal pairs of the 2-cent Black Jack of 1863, tied on cover by target cancels and Rochester, Jan. postmark to Buffalo, NY. With manuscript "Due 2" (probably 1 cent underpayment of triple 3 cent first class rate, plus 1 cent penalty). Pencil notation on reverse shows that this cover sold for $62.20 in a June, 1974 auction.

1-cent Columbian Exposition Issue: "Columbus in Sight of Land," issued Jan. 2, 1893. Retail value $12 mint, 20 cents used, $250 for plate block of six, $1500 for a first-day cover. The specimen shown is centered-to-bottom (CTB) and therefore grades very good because the perforations touch the design. Nearly 500 million printed!

In the autumn and winter of 1861, the Confederate States general issues replaced the upstart Provisionals. The general issue adhesives are collectible in their own right, some selling for hundreds of dollars each, and all serving to document the postal history of the embattled Confederacy as it struggled to carry its mails during the Civil War. Prisoner-of-war covers, covers from famous generals, cross-border covers ("per flag of truce"), and blockade-run covers are all prime Confederate items, the better ones bringing hundreds of dollars each at auction.

Condition of Confederate material is often awful due to the stressful circumstances under which it was made. Clean undamaged Confederate covers bring above average prices.

ENCASED POSTAGE STAMPS

What is the story behind encased postage stamps? How can you tell if they have been faked?

By the summer of 1862, uncertainty as to the outcome of the Civil War made many citizens hoard American coins out of circulation, starting with gold and silver, and then copper. Small change became so scarce that unused postage stamps began circulating among the public as an emergency substitute for coins.

John Gault, a young Boston entrepreneur, patented his "Design for Postage Stamp Case" with the U.S. Patent Office in July and August of 1862. Gault's device was brilliantly simple: a small circular brass frame enclosing an unused postage stamp whose face was visible through a mica window. Sold to merchants at two cents over face value, these "encased postage stamps" saw limited but immediate circulation.

Businesses had their names and towns embossed on the metal backs so that these encased stamps would carry their "advertising." Such commercial firms as "Drake's Plantation Bitters," "Ayer's Cathartic Pills," and "Lord & Taylor, New York" are known to have sponsored a number of different stamp denominations in these encased postage devices. When Gault moved his business to New York City, it became known as Kirkpatrick and Gault, and encased postage stamps with the slogans "J. Gault" and "Kirkpatrick & Gault" were produced.

Extensive fraud has been perpetrated on gullible collectors by manipulating these encased postage stamps to 1) replace cracked or scratched mica (pristine mica commands a premium value); 2) replace a low denomination stamp with a higher denomination (30-cent and 90-cent values sell for thousands of dollars each!); 3) clean the whole case so it looks more or less uncirculated. Any expensive encased postage stamp purchase absolutely must come with an expertizing certificate of authenticity, either from the Philatelic Foundation (preferably) or the American Philatelic Society. These are the two accepted authorities for U.S. stamps; write to them, asking for their latest expertizing fees and a stamp submission form (be sure to enclose a stamped, self-addressed #10 business envelope).

Expertizing

Philatelic Foundation
21 East 40th Street
New York, NY 10016

American Philatelic Society
P.O. Box 8000
State College, PA 16803

Retail and auction prices for undamaged encased postage stamps run from $100 to $300 for the cheaper items, $500 to $2,000 and up for the rarer varieties (scarce business names and/or high denomination encased stamps). They aren't unobtainable, but their true rarity is shown by the fact that many stamp dealers have no encased postage stamps in stock.

Chapter 8

Foreign Stamps

With a half million major varieties of foreign stamps listed in the standard catalogs, no book or person could ever hope to explore all of them with any degree of thoroughness. But we can pause and look at a few interesting foreign issues, selected as much for their beauty and historical significance as for their monetary worth.

Early Great Britain, Australian "kangaroos," popular Canadian issues, "dead" countries, Kennedy topicals, expedition adhesives, Hitler stamps, Russia, Denmark, Israel, the Falkland Islands, omnibus sets — all these are explained and examined in the following pages.

Many collectors begin the stamp hobby with a cheap album, a packet of hinges, and a couple of hundred colorful pictorial issues from around the world — stamps portraying African animals, tropical volcanoes, petty dictators, breathtaking landscapes, bizarre costumes, and local railway stations. But not all foreign stamps are as cheap as the ones in these beginner hobby kits.

FIRST BRITISH STAMPS

Could you give a brief history of the early Great Britain stamps? I believe they were called the Penny Black and 2-Pence Blue. I have a later version, a carmine-colored 1-penny stamp; does it have any value today?

Rowland Hill, a British subject, invented the postage stamp in 1840. In May of that year, the first adhesive stamps, a 1-penny black color and a 2-pence blue, were placed on sale in Great Britain. Bearing an engraved bust of the young Queen Victoria, the stamps were an immediate sensation and were readily accepted by the public as a convenient method of prepaying the postal fee on a letter. (The old custom was to collect the fee from the recipient.)

Today these first postage stamps sell for more than $1,000 each in choice mint condition. I recently attended a Los Angeles stamp auction where Penny Blacks sold for $100 each in nice cancelled condition. The 1-penny red brown (which you describe as carmine) retails for about $100 mint, $2 (and up) used if undamaged, and was issued a year later, in 1841, because black-ink cancels were hard to distinguish on the Penny Blacks, resulting in postage fraud by people who reused a cancelled Penny Black to mail another letter.

AUSTRALIAN "ROOS"

My Australian stamp pictures a kangaroo on a map of Australia, with the denomination of 2 pounds at the bottom. The color is reddish-pink and black. Can you tell me something about it?

This is one of the first issues of Australia proper (as distinct from Australian "states"), and is popular in both the U.S. and in its country of origin. Called the "Roos" in stamp collector talk, the "Kangaroo and Map" definitives of 1913-36 are eagerly sought after in the high denominations (2 shillings to 2 pounds).

Different printing varieties were made of the Roos, and the 2-pound value comes in various watermarks. A choice mint 2-pound Roo with full original gum sells for $1,000 or more; cancelled copies half of that and up, depending on the variety and condition. Centering and gum condition are all important in assessing the value of the Roos in the stamp market, which has experienced fluctuating prices for early Australian material. An off-center, damaged gum, dull color stamp may sell for 10-20% of the price of a superb copy.

EARLY CANADIAN ISSUES

When were the first Canadian stamps issued?

In 1851 a set of three Province of Canada stamps appeared in the post offices of our northern neighbor. They are very scarce in mint condition and sell for thousands of dollars each. From 1852 through 1859 Canada issued wove paper stamps that are also in high demand as mint copies or legitimately used on nice covers. Early Canadian stamps often have small margins and some kind of damage; pristine copies draw serious attention and money at auctions.

Which Canadian stamps are the most popular?

Besides the 19th century Queen Victoria material, the Jubilees of 1897 (similar to our Columbians in popularity), any pre-World War II dollar values as mint singles or blocks, some rare back-of-the-book items (like the 8-cent blue Registration stamp), imperf pairs, and unusual early commercial covers with high denominations or pretty combination frankings. The pre-1935 50-cent values are nice also in mint condition, as well as complete mint sets of the early 20th century definitives (like the Edward VII issues of 1903-08). If you buy all of the above you'll have a valuable collection.

What is a bluenose?

Either a frostbitten facial feature or the extremely beautiful 50-cent Canadian commemorative of 1929 portraying the Nova Scotia fishing and racing schooner, *Bluenose*. It was printed in a quantity of just over one million copies, many of which have seen postal duty, hence the moderate price of cancelled copies ($20 to $50). Choice mint examples go for $150 or more apiece, and mint blocks of the Bluenose are often the object of spirited bidding at auction.

What I like about it is its dark blue engraving, its simple but well-executed design with the ship at full sail pleasantly framed by a balanced assortment of artwork surrounding the vignette, and the semi-rare status making it affordable but at the same time desirable. A classic of 1920s era Canadian stamp production!

DEAD COUNTRIES

What is a dead country?

A nonexistent nation or political entity which once issued its own stamps that no longer does so. The great thing about dead countries is that their total stamp output (by individual varieties and sometimes even by quantities in press runs) is fixed and known, so it is possible to acquire a "complete" collection of major varieties. For a country long since "dead," there may be a lot of research in the form of handbooks and articles just waiting for you to enjoy. Some dead countries have the added attraction of not being the star performers in the latest round of speculative stamp market price booms and busts, so their prices are stable and maybe even affordable.

Privately issued blue colored trial proof the 25-cent rouletted "Yukon Airways & Exploration Co. Ltd" local post adhesive. A number of different Canadian labels such as this were popular on philatelic mail in the 1930s. Fully gummed with deliberately large margins.

Mixing franking of Canadian and U.S. stamps on piece. 7-cent Canadian "Geese in Flight" air mail, issued Sept. 16, 1946. U.S. Presidentials, 1-cent Washington (issued Jan. 20, 1939 as a coil perforated vertically) and 3-cent Jefferson (issued Jan. 20, 1939 as a coil). Cancelled Vancouver, Canada (British Columbia), July 9, 1951. Probably philatelically-inspired as U.S. postage wasn't valid in Canada.

4-cent Trans-Mississippi Exposition issue: "Indian Hunting Buffalo," issue date June 17, 1898. Two used copies, the one at left being a natural left-margin straight edge "on piece" with a Pittsburgh, Oct. 9, 1899 cancel; the right stamp is well-centered with a wavy line flag cancel of the time period. Retail price: $100 mint, $20 used, $1,200 for a plate number block of six. Issued in orange, notorious for turning brown due to oxidation over the years.

Some interesting dead countries are the former independent provinces of Canada which once issued their own stamps (like Newfoundland and Prince Edward Island), the Australian colonies (like Tasmania and New South Wales), the former separate parts of South Africa (Transvaal, Cape of Good Hope, etc.), and the ever changing political landscape of Europe (Danzig, Latvia, Prussia, Bavaria, Saar, etc.).

KENNEDY TOPICALS

I have an album of foreign stamps from many countries, all of the issues honoring the late President John F. Kennedy. Does this collection have any value?

Many nations flooded the market with memorial stamps when President Kennedy was assassinated, and today most of these issues are of nominal value. A large album full of different Kennedy issues, especially with souvenir sheets and covers, has some topical interest, but don't expect to get rich by selling it. Chances are that you don't have rare and expensive printing varieties, but show the stamps to a dealer for a professional opinion.

NEW ZEALAND EXPEDITIONS

I have a New Zealand 1-penny stamp with a "Victoria Land" overprint and a "British Antarctic Expedition Jan. 18th, 1913" cancellation. It is not listed in American catalogs. Do you know its background and value?

From 1908 to 1913 certain New Zealand stamps were taken on expeditions to Antarctica and used on mail and souvenir folders that were sent back to New Zealand. These stamps were not sold to the general public in post offices, so some catalogs dismiss them as lacking legitimate postal validity.

The Stanley Gibbons Stamp Catalogue (published by Stanley Gibbons Ltd. in Great Britain) says "these issues were made under authority of the New Zealand Postal Department and, while not strictly necessary, they actually franked correspondence to New Zealand. They were sold to the public at a premium."

I've seen these stamps auctioned at prices from $40 to $80 each. They're available in blocks, and sometimes the cancelled versions come on special expedition stationery with appropriate cancels, obviously made specifically for collectors.

RARE GERMAN CANCELS

How can a German stamp be worth twenty cents mint and $100 cancelled?

Some early German stamps are worth a great deal of money when found with genuine cancels because few authentic cancels are known, leading to extensive forging of cancels to raise the market price of a common mint stamp (let's hope the forger has enough sense to soak the gum off, too!). Demand for such rare cancels is high, hence their disproportionately high price compared to their mint counterparts.

It takes years of study of German stamps to become an expert on cancels. If you haven't done this research yourself, send the stamp to an expertizing service to verify the genuineness of the cancel, but only if the cost of expertizing ($10 or more) is worth the trouble, i.e., the stamp should have a high catalog value with a cancel.

HITLER STAMPS

I have a set of stamps with Hitler's picture on them, brought back in 1945 from Germany. They are still new and uncancelled. Do they have a lot of value?

Probably not. The Reich postal authorities issued millions of stamps with the Nazi dictator's portrait, and only a few rare varieties are worth more than a few cents each today. A standard stamp catalog at your local library or a quick visit to any stamp shop will help you determine if you have rare or common "Hitler heads" as they are called.

RUSSIAN STAMPS

How much are modern Russian stamps worth?

About as much as the paper they're printed on, if they're issues from the last thirty years. The Soviet Union releases a flood of stamps every year, and recent ones are of no special value. This isn't true for some early pre-Revolution Russian stamps or the rarer air mails of the 1930s.

I once traded stamps by mail with a collector in the Ukraine. He was a doctor in a coal mining town and sent me special Soviet cancels in exchange for whatever I could send to him. Once I mailed a selection of old Russian stamps from the early 20th century, and he replied in his next letter that the members of his stamp club were quite excited to see these obsolete Russian issues that they have a hard time finding in the Soviet Union.

The U.S.S.R., by the way, actively encourages stamp collecting, but it is not as freewheeling or as commercial as it is in the United States. Chairman Gorbachev might change a few things, but most Russian collectors still have difficulty getting foreign catalogs and early rare stamps of any country.

DANISH STAMPS

I have all the stamps issued by Denmark since 1960. They are in perfect condition, and I would like to know their value.

Nothing is in "perfect" condition, but assuming that your Danish collection consists of mint, never hinged, full original gum, full perforations, and very fine centering for *all* of the issues since 1960, then the current retail price might be about $250.

THE FIRST ISRAELI STAMPS

What are the most desirable Israeli stamps?

From a financial standpoint, the three high values (250-Mils, 500-Mils, and 1000-Mils) of the 1948 Ancient Judean Coin issue. This trio sells for $300 to $500 as a group, and with "tabs" the price is $2,000 to $4,000. The condition is all important on early (1948) Israeli issues. The climate and political-economic upheavals in that country over the years have not always been kind to stamp preservation. Tropical stains, damaged gum, and other problems will reduce the value of any first-issue Israeli stamp.

WORLDWIDE COLLECTIONS

I have a general worldwide collection of stamps from the 1940s which I accumulated by spending my twenty-five cents a week allowance for several years. Could these issues have value?

They could, but they probably don't. A young person's allowance in the 1940s would not have bought valuable stamps, unless you were lucky enough to get, for instance, some of the western European stamps with small printings or the Japanese souvenir sheets at face value. A standard catalog or stamp dealer can help you to evaluate your collection.

But the stamps have sentimental value, don't they? I'll bet you can remember where you got many of them, and interesting memories of your early collecting years are worth more than the stamps could ever be! If you're tired of the collection and it has no special meaning to you, why don't you give it to some young person and inspire another stamp collector?

FALKLAND ISLANDS

Are the Falkland Islands still as popular to collect as they were a few years ago?

Yes, especially the pre-1935 issues, although some of the better Falklands fluctuate in price with the general stamp market. With a permanent resident population of less than 2,000, the Falkland Islands have a fascinating history and a stark primitive beauty all their own.

You may remember the Argentine-British war that flared up in the Falklands in the early 1980s. Covers with cancels that reflect those skirmishes are nice late 20th century Falklands postal history. A British Crown Colony, the Falklands are also claimed by Argentina which calls them the Malvinas. Argentina even issued a 20,000-Pesos (inflation!) commemorative stamp in 1983 to promote the "Recovery of the Malvinas."

Island nations with curious stamps, particularly if they have small printings, have a romantic popularity among collectors. Try finding the 1917 set of Postage Dues from Fiji. Or Bahamas issues from the 1860s on original covers. Or any of the pre-1860 stamps from the island of Mauritius. Talk about intrigue! Talk about investment value!

OMNIBUS ISSUES

What is an omnibus issue?

An omnibus issue refers to stamps of common design or having a certain theme, issued by many different countries which may or may not be closely associated with each other politically. For example, the Europa issues of Western Europe; the 1939 (150th anniversary) French Revolution issues of a couple of dozen French colonies; and the 1948-49 Silver Wedding stamps of dozens of British colonies.

An omnibus issue is a topical specialty that allows a collector to collect the world for a narrowly defined commemorative purpose. Some dealers buy and sell the more popular omnibus sets as a whole group, mint, with wholesale and retail prices plainly stated.

BRITISH COMMON-WEALTH SPECIALTIES

How can anyone collect the entire British Commonwealth of present and former possessions? Over 200 separate postal administrations!

British Empire stamps are a significant portion of all the stamps ever issued by the world's postal authorities. Nobody seriously collects the entire British Commonwealth anymore, but there are many appealing specialties:

(1) *Single reign issues*, i.e., restricting yourself to the stamps produced during the reign of Queen Elizabeth (QEII in collector slang) or Edward VIII.

(2) *Single countries*, like Kenya, Bermuda, or Cyprus.

(3) *Subdivisions of a country*, like the Native Feudatory States of India or the Dependencies of New Zealand (like Cook Islands or Western Samoa).

(4) *A single stamp* like the Penny Black of Great Britain or a common early definitive of Canada.

(5) *Boer War covers* or other specialized postal history of British colonies.

(6) *Covers and cancels from foreign countries*, like the British "Offices in Morocco."

(7) *Regional British* issues like the recent Guernsey, Northern Ireland, or Scotland definitives.

Chapter 9

Defects and Damage

Creases, stains, pinholes, disturbed gum, bent or missing perforation teeth, pencil and pen marks, common dirt — all horrors straight out of a philatelist's nightmare — are dealt with in this chapter.

The ethics of stamp cleaning and repairing is a subject that comes up over and over again in the articles and "letters to the editor" pages of the stamp hobby newspapers. The basic rule is to alter a stamp or cover as little as possible. Try to make all repairs reversible in case the results are undesirable for one reason or another. And *never* misrepresent a philatelic item when offering it for sale. It is perfectly legal to clean, repair, and buy or sell such "doctored up" stamps and covers. It is illegal and completely inexcusable morally to offer for sale anything that has hidden defects which the prospective purchaser would definitely like to know about if only you were honest enough to point out the flaws in your merchandise. If you need to cheat people to make a quick buck, then you need more than money to make your life worthwhile.

But countless stamps and covers *are* damaged to some extent. What can we do about it?

CREASES *Can a crease be removed from a stamp? Some of my older stamps are lightly creased, and I know that this detracts from their value.*

Creases tend to be permanent because once the stamp's paper fibers are broken, they stay broken. Careful pressing under a stack of books or *delicate* ironing with a *slightly* warm iron over a creased stamp sandwiched between thin cardboard (like file folders) will sometimes help, but you always run the risk of further damaging the stamp.

Creased stamps are collectible, and many of the most sought-after rarities are creased, but any crease does reduce a stamp's market value. The more prominent the crease, the lower the value. Honest collectors and dealers buy and sell creased stamps all the time and describe them as such during the transactions. Watermark fluid will often reveal a crease that an unscrupulous stamp "doctor" has tried to hide.

STAINS *Can stains be removed from stamps?*

That depends on the type of chemical that caused the stain. Usually it is best to leave the stamp alone or sell it rather than trying to remove a stain with anything other than plain tap water. The stamp weeklies (Chapter 1) sometimes carry ads from "stamp restoring" services, although you risk losing both the stamp and some money if their treatment doesn't work. I think that if a soaking for several hours in water doesn't affect the stain, then you need the help of a paper restoration expert.

RUST SPOTS *I have heard that if you soak a stamp off its envelope paper in cold water and then lift it out with stamp tongs, there is a possibility that the metal tongs will leave a rust spot on the stamp. Is that correct?*

Unlikely, *unless* the tongs were already rusted before you used them to remove the soaked-off stamp. Most stamp tongs are made of nickel-plated or stainless steel, and the brief encounter between tongs and a wet stamp would hardly be long enough to start a rust reaction. You don't let the tongs stay wet, do you? Stainless steel *will* rust if it is kept wet, so thoroughly dry your tongs with paper towels (not cloth, paper works better) after dipping them in water.

PINHOLES *If a stamp has a pinhole in it, does that destroy its value?*

Usually. The bigger the hole and the closer it is to the center of the stamp's design, the less the value of the stamp. Many collectors won't even look at a stamp with a hole, unless it is a great rarity, and even then it will be heavily discounted from its normal (sound) price.

Expect holes from the staples in the selvage (margin paper) of booklet panes or of plate blocks (if the stamp panes were originally stapled together as shipped from the printer). Believe it or not, in the early years of stamp collecting, the mid-19th century, dealers had the habit of *pinning* stamps to their display boards. When a customer wanted to buy a stamp, he pointed to it and the dealer unpinned it, a source of some of the pinholes in classic stamps.

Expect pinholes near the centers of old envelopes because they were temporarily filed on spindle needles in offices. For rare covers, a tiny pinhole is not a major problem and may even be one of the many marks of authenticity.

Expect pinholes on old checks and other small legal documents, but don't buy them if the hole goes through any revenue stamps attached. An interesting specialty that comes and goes in popularity is the collecting of revenue stamps on old (19th and early 20th century) bank checks.

DISTURBED GUM   *What does disturbed gum mean? I see advertisements selling old stamps with disturbed gum.*

Gum is the "glue" put on the backs of stamps to facilitate licking and sticking on envelopes. It is a brilliant chemical invention and has been on the backs of most stamps since the first ones in Great Britain in May 1840.

Because collectors and investors pay so much more money for certain stamps with undisturbed gum, the state of the gum on a stamp becomes an important question. When the gum is found to be as issued, with no damage visible, it is called original gum, never hinged (OGNH).

Gum can be disturbed by a stamp hinge, licking, humidity from the atmosphere, mold, chemical stains, by touching with fingers, or by being scratched or cracked by some natural or artificial means. Gum may be glazed, spotted, partial, or totally lacking on a stamp that once had it. Forgers with an eye to larceny sometimes put faked gum on a stamp to make it appear mint and therefore more valuable. There are laboratories in Europe that openly advertise their services in regumming stamps for collectors!

My advice is to buy a stamp with clean gum, lightly hinged, at catalog prices or a slight discount from catalog (for most stamps). Get never hinged, undisturbed gum when possible, but don't pay a fortune for it because. . .

Herman Herst, Jr., the famous New York stamp dealer now retired in Florida, says that half or more of U.S. 19th century stamps that appear to be mint with flawless original gum are in reality regummed fakes, or at best are highly suspect as to their "undisturbed" gum. The obvious source of original gum stamps is multiples: blocks or full panes of 19th century stamps, with some of the stamps (often the lower ones due to album placing) having never been hinged. Because hinging was the rule rather than the exception in stamp collecting in the late 19th and early 20th century, it is ironic that a mint stamp with hinged gum may be your best assurance that the gum is indeed original, having spent years as a hinged specimen in some old-time collection.

A fellow collector is offering to sell a $5 Columbian mint commemorative to me for $300. Is this a good deal? The stamp looks perfect.

Nothing is perfect in philately or in any other field of collectibles, but I think that this stamp is either damaged or a counterfeit. Or perhaps your friend doesn't keep up to date with stamp values. A $5 mint Columbian in extremely fine condition (well-centered with original gum) currently sells for several thousand dollars at retail.

Inspect the stamp with a magnifier for evidence of regumming, sealed tears (try watermark fluid), erased cancels, and recut perforations. And if you don't trust your judgment, let a stamp dealer look at it. The U.S. Postal Inspection Service, discussing mail order fraud, states: "If it looks too good to be true, it probably is!" Purported perfection, far from making you relaxed and happy, should make you triply suspicious when examining an expensive or rare stamp.

DAMAGED PERFORATIONS

How do I correct bent or missing perforation teeth?

The missing ones are gone forever, but with a little care and a steady hand, you may be able to straighten out a bent perf with tongs. Lay the stamp flat on a surface and *slowly* move the bent perf to its original position; be careful not to break it off. Flatten the unfolded perf under the weight of books for several days.

**CLEANING
AND PROTECTING
PHILATELIC ITEMS**

How do I clean the dirt off of old envelopes? Some of them date from the 1880s and have been in our family since then. How can I remove pencil and pen marks?

All paper ages with the passage of time. Some discoloration and brittleness is inevitable, but you can usually remove unsightly pencil marks on envelopes by *gently* rubbing them with a good soft pencil eraser (not the ones on pencils, but the lozenge-shaped pink ones that you used in grade school). The trick is to be conservative and cautious when erasing the pencil markings: be sure that you don't tear or wrinkle the envelope or further stain the paper with the eraser's trace.

Ink marks are close to impossible to eradicate completely, either mechanically or chemically, and attempts to rub out 19th-century iron-based inks or modern ball point inks often leave the paper with unpleasant "cleaning zones" on it. *Ink eradicator* chemicals sold in stationery stores might work on some inks to a certain extent, but practice on an unimportant piece of paper before you tackle the ink removal on a treasured cover.

Paper restoration is a science in which experience is priceless. If this is your first envelope cleaning, expect average to poor results. Talk to your librarian for advice on paper preservation or for books on the subject.

Stamp and cover damage is easier prevented than remedied, and the best ways to protect stamp collections are by storing them in cool (not cold) dark surroundings with average humidity (not too high or too dry), away from paper-eating insects and mold spores, away from dust and chemical fumes, and with a little ventilation to keep the air circulating.

I often wondered how museums could keep old things in choice condition in the heat and humidity of the summer months, and the answer is that they can't. More and more museums that display art objects, including old manuscripts and documents, are installing climate-control systems in their exhibition galleries. Have you seen the little thermometers and humidity gauges inside the glass cases showing the artifacts from King Tut's tomb?

Bank vault safe deposit boxes are excellent places for keeping the stamps that have monetary or sentimental value because most bank vaults have some measure of climate control, and at least don't experience the frequent wide temperature or humidity swings found in your home every day.

LEGITIMATE VS. UNETHICAL STAMP REPAIRS

What are the ethics of making stamp repairs?

Washing a stamp in water, erasing pencil marks on covers, straightening a bent perf, gluing a detached stamp back on its envelope in its *original* position, and reinforcing separated perfs on blocks with hinges are all acceptable repairs. Regumming, adding pieces of paper to a stamp or cover, tracing over a cancel or postal marking to make it more visible, hiding thins with hinges, reperforating (including adding perfs to straight edges that never had them), and finding a stamp that *could* have been on a cover that is missing one — all of these "repairs" are done daily and are *not ethical* from my viewpoint; there is too great a risk that a novice collector won't recognize an excellent repair job, and pay more for the item than it is worth in its damaged state.

In other words, *cleaning* and *protecting* philatelic material are necessary acts, but extravagant restoration projects border on the fraudulent. And obviously any repairs *must* be stated by the seller when such stamps are sold. I disagree with dealers who say "let the buyer beware." An ethical dealer points out everything when either buying or selling, and with all of the philatelic cards on the negotiating table, everybody can make informed decisions. Or is repeat business not worth having?

DEFECTS AND VALUES

What effect does a defect have on philatelic values?

If you mean monetary values, a lot! Every item must be individually evaluated because of the uniqueness of defects (are any two cover stains *exactly* alike?), but here are some rough guide lines for price discounting when buying defective merchandise:

If a stamp is worth a retail price of $100 for superb mint, original gum, never hinged, as "flawless" as they come, then this table might apply to its damaged cousins:

THE EFFECT OF "DEFECTS" ON THE RETAIL PRICE OF A HYPOTHETICAL POSTAGE STAMP	
The Stamp's Condition	**Retail Value**
Superb, OG, NH (Superb, original gum, never hinged)	$100.00
Very Fine, OG, LH (lightly hinged)	60.00
Fine, Unused, NG (no gum)	40.00
Fine, Unused, RG (regummed)	40.00 (if the dealer is honest)
Fine, Unused, NG, small tropical stains ("foxing" in rare manuscript talk)	25.00 (if the stamp is popular)
Fine, Unused, NG, straightedge along one side	20.00
Fine, Unused, NG, missing a few perfs in prominent positions	20.00
Fine, Unused, NG, TTH (tiny thin)	15.00
Fine, Unused, NG, small pinhole in the stamp's design	15.00 (or less)
Fine, Unused, NG, *and* one of the following: major thin, piece of stamp missing, severe surface scrape, heavy hinge remnant obviously covering some defect, badly discolored	5.00 (if that much) to 10.00

Fine in this chart refers to centering. A stamp that is damaged is not fine overall, but very good to poor. And realize that discriminating philatelists may not want a defective stamp at any price. The above table applies *if* you can find a buyer!

One more thing about thins. The larger the area that a thin covers on a stamp, or the deeper the penetration of the thin, or the nearer the thin is to the stamp's center, the less valuable the stamp. Don't confuse normal watermarks with thinning defects; they sometimes look alike in watermark fluid.

Chapter 10

Errors

Errors! Just say the word and watch a philatelist's eyes light up! Who hasn't dreamed of finding a rare stamp error? Of being handed an imperforate pane of stamps at the post office? Of receiving a missing color adhesive on an envelope in the morning's mail? Of discovering a double overprint or an upside down airplane in a shoe box of junk stamps?

Errors are of several types, major and minor, and this chapter explores some of the popular ones.

BLIND PERFS *I have five pairs of what appear to be unperforated 8-cent Eisenhower stamps. There are slight indentations on the reverse sides where five of the perforation holes should be. What are these?*

A printing oddity, not a major error. If any of the "indentations" (collectors call them "blind perforations") are visible between two stamps that were normally issued with perforation holes, then you cannot call them genuine imperforate varieties, and their value as errors drops sharply. All imperforate pairs of U.S. stamps retail from $5 up, with many costing hundreds of dollars. Your blind perforated Eisenhower stamps are worth maybe $1 per pair. Use a magnifying glass so that you *never* pay imperf prices for blind perfs.

EFO CLUB *Is there a national organization that studies errors?*

Yes, the Errors, Freaks and Oddities Collectors Club publishes the bimonthly journal *EFO Collector*, and sponsors sales circuits, expertizing service, study groups, and exhibition awards. Dues are $10 per year. Send a self-addressed stamped envelope for a membership application to:

Errors, Freaks and Oddities Collectors Club
1903 Village Road West
Norwood, MA 02062

A selection of post-World War II U.S. air mails, issued 1946 through 1961. Retail value: not much more than face for mint singles, $3 each for plate blocks of four of the 4-cent "Eagle in Flight" and the 13-cent "Liberty Bell." Over 100 major varieties of U.S. air mail stamps have been released since the first in 1918.

15- cent misperforation ("shifted perfs") Oliver Wendell Holmes coil definitive with normal copy at right. Value of the error: $1 or $2. Issue date: June 14, 1978 as a coil in the Prominent Americans definitive issue. Imperforate pairs are known of this stamp.

Imperforate pair of 20-cent coil definitives "Flag Over Supreme Court" of Dec. 17, 1981. Many of these errors have been found, hence the retail price of only $4.50 per pair. Also known with black and blue colors omitted.

Are there more imperforate errors these days? It seems that every time I look at a stamp magazine I see new imperf errors being discovered.

There does appear to be more stamp errors in general being released by the Postal Service since the 1960s — as compared to what was discovered in the postal paper produced by the old Post Office Department. Whatever the reasons, whether it is busy work schedules, more complex printing processes, malfunctioning equipment, poor quality control, pilferage by postal workers of printer's waste, or confusing press runs of ever-changing issue designs, there are definitely more and more production errors and oddities being found in current U.S. stamps.

PRICE OF ERRORS

What determines the price of errors? Does it pay to sell them immediately or hold onto to them for years?

Like all stamps, supply and demand determine the market price of errors. When a major error is just discovered, usually by somebody buying it at a post office, it can initially be worth hundreds of dollars (for an imperf pair) or thousands of dollars (like the "CIA" $1 Americana Candle Holder invert) each. *If no more* copies of the error are ever found, the market price tends to stay stable or even rise a bit with the passage of time. *If many more are found*, the market value usually crashes through the floor.

So speaking practically, if you are fortunate enough to run across a real stamp error at the post office, you have to decide whether to sell now or hold for a while. And because nobody can foresee the future, this dilemma is not easy to resolve. By asking around, investigating whether any more are known, and by showing your newly captured error to an error specialist dealer, you can get a rough idea of the relative scarcity of a new error.

PLATE SMEARS

What are plate smears?

Plate smears are ink that wasn't completely wiped off of the printing plate when the stamp was being printed, resulting in a patch of ink (of varying degrees of disfigurement) where it shouldn't be on the stamp's surface. Plate smears aren't major varieties, and are worth only a nominal amount of money, maybe a few dollars each at the most (over face value).

ERROR DEALERS   *Are there dealers who specialize in stamp errors?*

Yes, and three well-known dealers who buy and sell major errors are:

> Jacques C. Schiff, Jr., Inc.
> 195 Main Street
> Ridgefield Park, NJ 07660

> J. Nalbandian, Inc.
> P.O. Box A, Pilgrim Station
> Warwick, RI 02888

> Marvin Frey
> 2199 Legion Street
> Bellmore, NY 11710

All three are members of the American Stamp Dealer's Association (ASDA) and the American Philatelic Society (APS). All have been in business for a number of years, know the stamp error market, and try to be fair whether buying or selling. Write to them if you have a major error to buy or sell. And, of course, I have no personal financial interest in their companies; I just recommend them as reliable error dealers.

Jacques C. Schiff, Jr. is the most famous stamp error dealer in the United States, and he writes columns on this subject for the stamp weeklies. Marvin Frey will buy even minor errors that he needs for his stock. Write before sending them stamps in the mail.

5-CENT COLOR ERROR   *I have one of the 5-cent color error stamps of 1917. What is its value today?*

The story goes that because of overwork due to World War I printing needs, the Bureau of Engraving and Printing (BEP) accidentally used a 5-cent transfer roll for reentry work on a 2-cent stamp plate. Carmine (a shade of red) was the normal color for 2-cent stamps at that time, and blue for 5-centers. So when the error plate was printed, it had 5-cent carmine stamps mixed in with the normal 2-cent carmines.

These 5-cent carmine errors were printed in March 1917, and were shipped out to post offices without the color mistake being noted by postal personnel. Some were undoubtedly thrown into wastebaskets after being received in a cancelled state on envelopes, others have been lost over the years through mildew, neglect, and any of the other enemies of paper. And since they were a bit scarce to begin with, they now sell for hundreds of dollars each.

Most collectors like to get this error attached next to the normal 2-cent examples, in blocks with the middle stamps being the color errors. $500 is a typical price for such a block of nine stamps (the middle one being the color error). And if you are lucky enough to have the 5-cent carmine on an envelope, properly cancelled from that time period, you have a $1,000 item! (But don't forget *condition*.)

COLOR ERRORS
I've heard that the 10-cent Man-on-the-Moon issue has an expensive color error. Is this true?

Yes! The "First Man on the Moon" U.S. air mail 10-cent stamp from 1969 is known with the lithographed rose-red color missing. Value? $250 each, retail price.

But beware of fakes. On authentic errors of this stamp, the red is missing from the entire picture — the dots above the yellow areas as well as from the astronaut's shoulder patch. Some unscrupulous people have learned how to bleach out the colors of certain stamps. Buy expensive errors only from reliable dealers who guarantee a refund if the stamp should later prove to be a forgery or fake. And when you're suspicious, insist on an expertizing certificate from the APS or PF (see Chapter 13).

What is the Columbian color error?

The 4-cent value of the U.S. Columbian Exposition Issue of 1893 is known with a blue color error instead of the usual ultramarine. This blue error normally sells for $2,000 to $4,000 mint, but *beware* of altered color: I would never buy this stamp without an expertizing certificate because it is easy to chemically alter a stamp's color.

And if you're not an observant stamp collector, you probably won't recognize the normal ultramarine shade of the stamp anyway.

POSTAL CARDS

I have two postal cards. One shows the full stamp and part of another of the 3-cent Statue of Liberty. The other card is an upside-down 2-cent Franklin. I have been unable to locate any reference to these two cards. What is their value?

Your 3-cent card is a double impression, selling at retail for about $200 mint. The 2-cent card is miscut, probably by a collector or dealer who was playing a joke or wanted to make some fast money by creating an instant faked "inverted" impression error. The 2-cent card has no special value; it was created by someone obtaining a full sheet of mint cards and cutting them to simulate an inverted design.

What was the "Garbage card"?

In 1902 a few postal cards with a "full face" view of the recently assassinated (in 1901) President McKinley were produced and imprinted with the address of a "trash" company, hence their nickname, the "Garbage cards." Auction value: $1,000 and up, with mint undefaced cards worth more than company imprinted or cancelled cards.

Later on, during the summer of 1902, the "normal" version of the card with a side view of McKinley appeared in post offices, and is now worth a couple of dollars mint, a few cents cancelled. The "Garbage card" obviously was never intended for general distribution, and although it has major catalog status, some philatelists consider it to be somewhat of an "error."

CANCEL DATE ERRORS

How many mistakes are made annually with postage meter machines? I sometimes receive metered mail with the wrong dates or wrong years, like "May 38, 1989" or "July 3, 1997."

Impossible dates and mail that arrives years early or late are the by-product of deliberate or inadvertent settings on office postage meter machines. Because these mistakes are common and easily prepared, they are not in demand and have no special value as errors. Anyone with access to a postage meter machine in a business office mailing room can custom make any date desired. If a so-called error is easy to forge (like single stamp imperforates or no-gum varieties), then it is avoided by serious stamp collectors.

Sometimes the Postal Service makes an error in the dating

slugs of their cancelling machines. Upside-down numbers, dates in the past or future, and total lack of date appear from time to time in official Postal Service cancellations. These are usually worthless also, although certainly curious and often startling!

MIS-REGISTERED COLORS

I have a U.S. commemorative stamp with a kind of "ghost effect" of two portraits superimposed on each other, i.e., the person in the stamp's design has four eyes, two mouths, and two noses. Are these errors valuable?

Probably not. It sounds like you have a slight mis-registration of colors, a common printing variety with modern photogravure equipment. Color mis-registrations are unlisted in the standard general stamp catalogs which try to mention all known major printing errors of stamps. A major printing error is an imperforate pair (if the normal type is perforated), striking color difference, entirely missing color(s), inverted frame or vignette (border or central design), and wrong paper or wrong watermark. Major errors are valuable, minor errors are not. All errors have a market, just be realistic when trying to sell a block of stamps that are perforated a few millimeters off center.

What does "printed on both sides" mean?

This means that the stamp is truly printed on both sides of the paper, with a *normal* orientation for the design on both sides. Don't confuse this with *offset* impressions with one side (the "back") having a *backwards* design, caused by ink adhering to adjacent sheets of stamps when they are stacked and still wet from the printer. Offset impressions are printing oddities worth little, but printed on both sides can be quite valuable, as in the case of the U.S. Civil War 2-cent Black Jack stamp, selling for $15 to $30 for average centered cancelled specimens, but worth several thousand dollars when printed on both sides.

WATERMARK ERRORS

Give an example of a watermark error.

A popular and well-known one is the $1 Woodrow Wilson 1938 Presidential definitive which was printed in a small quantity on U.S. Internal Revenue paper in 1951, causing the "USIR" watermark to appear on these stamps, now worth about $200 mint, $50 used per stamp, compared to maybe $6 mint and a few cents used for the unwatermarked normal version.

Another is the 1-penny carmine King Edward VII Transvaal definitive of 1907 with an Anchor watermark of the Cape of Good Hope; cancelled copies sell for high three-figure prices, as opposed to a few cents for the normal "Multiple Crown and C.A." watermark of Transvaal.

Chapter 11

Investing in Stamps

How to select a stamp for investment, the factors of condition-supply-demand, wholesale vs. retail prices, market cycles, catalog values in relation to actual market prices, overpaying, first-day covers, plate blocks and sheets, the Graf Zeppelins, "investment" rackets, dealing with dealers, stamp storage, and collection appraisals are discussed in this chapter.

Knowledge is power and it is urgently necessary when investment dollars are on the table. Indeed, some stamp specialists suggest that investors stay away from stamps completely because the market is so unpredictable and often long in changing; others advise to buy recklessly and hope for the best.

My philosophy is to be a collector first, and an investor second. And when serious money is laid out, be certain that you are getting top value for your hard-earned cash. Choice stamps, carefully selected as to price and condition, tend to increase in value over the years. But you have to do your philatelic homework.

MARKET CYCLES   *Are stamps a good investment in the next few years?*

The rare stamp market has been price depressed since the auction and retail highs reached during the winter of 1979-80. The selective national economic recession of the early 1980s, which has now ended, had a big impact on stamp collectors and philatelic investors. Many rare U.S. and foreign stamps are now selling for half of what they brought at auction in 1980.

Some stamp dealers have gone bankrupt, and many ill-informed stamp speculators have bailed out of the stamp market since 1980, taking major financial losses on their over-promoted or overpriced stamps that were bought at the height of the stamp boom around 1980. Some dealers and investors are therefore disillusioned about the prospects of stamp profits at the present time.

Bernard Baruch, the Wall Street wizard, had some excellent advice when asked how to make money in the stock market. He replied that his investment philosophy was to buy when others are selling, and sell when others are buying. By going against the trend of a changing market, you have a chance to get things at bargain prices and sell them at a nice profit while others are feverishly buying during the boom phase.

Stamp prices follow cycles like everything else in a free economy. Philatelic values now are universally recognized to be bargains compared to what they were and to what they might become. The present time seems right to buy carefully selected quality stamps that *are not* damaged or overpriced to begin with. When inflation heats up again, as it has a good chance of doing in the 1990s, stamp prices will inevitably follow the rising costs of the national economy in general.

In other words, choice stamps are probably good to buy for the long term, looking five or ten years ahead.

COLLECTORS, SPECULATORS, AND INVESTORS

You seem to give contradictory advice. On the one hand you say rare stamps retain their value. Then you point out that stamps can drop in price, and there is no certain way to predict when this will happen or which issues will be affected. Why are stamps a logical investment?

Because by studying the long-term stamp market you can see trends and anticipate long-range effects of the changing market prices of rare stamps. The best *investor* in stamps or any rare collectible hard asset item (coins, art, gold, antiques, etc.) is a *collector*, not a *speculator*.

Speculators are people who buy something and hope it will go up in price fast so they can make a quick giant profit. It is a rare individual who makes money speculating in stamps because too many unknowable factors govern stamp prices: collecting fads, government postal policies, the discovery of hoards or the auctioning of previously unknown stamps, the state of the economy in general, etc.

Investors are people who study a commodity market very carefully, then cautiously invest a *portion* of their surplus funds in carefully selected items chosen for their good track record in price appreciation over the years, such as a blue chip stock on Wall Street.

Collectors appreciate the material first, and the profits (if any) only second. Yet it is funny how collectors seem to make higher profits than many investors and most speculators. A true collector knows what is rare and beautiful and knows what other collectors like and want. Collecting is emotional and might be considered a sort of higher instinct in human beings, so it stands to reason that a well-planned and prudently acquired collection of choice and rare material will always appeal to other collectors who specialize in such items.

The investors who got "burned" in the past maybe neglected their homework. A lot of time and effort is required to get to know a selected group of stamps — the knowledge that enables you to invest intelligently in them. If you know what is good, and if you know that the selling price is sensible at this time in history, then you are well on your way to being a successful investor.

If there was any shortcut to stamp investing, we would all be rich. The challenge is to study the market and buy nice stamps for the long term!

CONDITION,
SUPPLY, AND DEMAND

My father gave me a stamp collection when I was a little boy. The U.S. issues go back to 1890, and there are many nice foreign examples from the 19th century, including Austria, Belgium, Denmark, and France. I tried to sell this collection to a local dealer, and he wouldn't even look through the book. How can hundred-year-old stamps be valueless? I find it hard to believe that my irreplaceable collection is of no worth.

Your story is a perfect example of tales told daily by people who wish to get some money from an old family stamp collection. Condition, supply, and demand are the factors that determine stamp market values. Many old stamps are indeed close to worthless because of the tremendous quantities printed then which are still readily available today; because poor condition makes the stamps undesirable to discriminating philatelists with cash to spend; and because collecting fads and traditions declare that the stamps in question are unpopular.

The 3-cent rose Washington regular issue of 1861 is worth maybe a quarter or fifty cents uncancelled, and that's only in nice condition with full perforations and no damage (tears, stains, etc.). Hundreds of millions of this stamp were issued by the U.S. Post Office Department in the 1860s, and most stamp dealers today have stock books full of them. On the other hand, a rare error made last year might sell for hundreds of dollars, so date alone means nothing in stamp prices. A knowledgeable dealer will not tell you that your stamps are worthless if they are valuable. Go to another dealer; if your stamps are truly of value, someone will eventually recognize it.

WHOLESALE AND RETAIL PRICES

What is the difference between wholesale and retail prices? Whenever I go to sell stamps, dealers seem to want to offer me a lot less than I think my stuff is worth. But when they sell to me, they insist on top dollar. Why are they so greedy for money from the people who support their businesses?

Dealers have to make a profit to keep their efforts financially worthwhile. A full-time stamp dealer has an enormous overhead in the business: advertising expenses, store rent or table fees at stamp shows, insurance, the money tied up in buying the stock, salaries of employees, taxes, utilities, mailing costs, etc. From their profits derive all the personal income of the dealers.

Could *you* buy a stamp for $10, sell it for $12 and from the $2 profit pay your business overhead and have enough left over to care for your family? The world has many kinds of people. I like to think that most professional stamp dealers are ethical businesspersons who buy and sell at fair prices. About 50% of retail is a rough guide for a wholesale dealer buying price for an average stamp, but many factors influence the price of stamps.

CATALOG VALUES ONLY A ROUGH GUIDE

My stamp collection consists of mostly mint Canadian stamps with a total catalog value of about $900. What would a dealer pay me if I sold today?

That depends on which issues you have and their conditions. Catalog values are quite meaningless without knowing which stamps are involved.

One stamp (like the $1 mint Canadian Jubilee of 1897) in superb condition and worth $900 alone is usually much more desirable than a hundred stamps (like the first Canadian air mail of 1928, the 5-cent "Allegory of Flight") worth $9 apiece. If your stamps are damaged (tears, folds, missing perforations, stains, disturbed gum), their market value crashes through the floor regardless of catalog value.

Also, if you have dozens of copies of the same stamp, a small-time dealer might not want to tie up a lot of capital in a huge stock of the identical issue that may take years to sell off. But if you have choice mint or used Canadian stamps cataloging $50 or more each, many dealers would be delighted to look at them.

As a very rough rule, if the stamps catalog $900, a dealer might buy them for $200 or $300, and sell them for $500 or $600. Few stamps sell for full catalog value because catalog prices have traditionally been inflated, not to fool anybody, but just to carry on the custom. It makes collectors happy when they can buy a stamp at a discount off catalog price.

Why is it possible to buy almost any stamp at auction for a third to a fifth off the catalog price? Are catalog values normally over retail prices?

Yes, in many cases. Compiling thousands of stamp prices in an annual catalog (like Scott, Minkus, or Gibbons) is a monumental job. The catalog editors must scan many price lists from retail stamp dealers and average out numerous auction prices before coming to a conclusion on the catalog value for a given stamp. To complicate matters, stamps in different conditions can sell for drastically different prices, so much subjective judgment is involved before deciding on whether to change the catalog price or leave it the same as in last year's edition. Beginning with the 1990 catalogs, Scott Publishing Company, the recognized authority on stamp catalog values in the United States, will list retail prices instead of the traditional inflated price quotes.

Catalogs also tend to overprice stamps because their authors anticipate a rising demand or inflation in the many months between the time that the catalog prices are collated and the publication date of the catalog. Like science textbooks, a stamp catalog is outdated the day it is released, but it is merely meant as a general guide to stamp market values, not a financial bible with unchangeable and absolutely correct philatelic values.

MODERN SHEETS *I have hundreds of sheets of mint stamps that I bought from the post office in the last fifteen years. I've been told that my sheets are a poor investment, and that I should tear off the plate number block of four from each sheet, and use the rest for postage on my mail. Or should I sell the sheets intact and buy silver as an investment?*

I can't guarantee the future values of stamps, a subject that I know something about. I know nothing about silver bullion, except that its market price has varied from $5 to almost $50 per ounce over the last dozen years. Nobody knows for sure what stamps or silver or anything else will definitely be worth in ten years.

You don't mention the denomination of your stamps, but assuming that you have hundreds of panes (what most people call "sheets"), *and* that each pane has seventy-five stamps to it (most panes have fifty or a hundred stamps in the United States), *and* that all of your stamps have a face value of 18 cents each (the average U.S. first class postal rate of the last fifteen years), *then* your stamps have a face value of $13.50 per pane, or $1,350 per hundred panes, or $13,500 per thousand panes.

It is true that common U.S. post office panes of stamps have been poor investments. In fact, most of the U.S. commemorative and definitive (regular) stamps of the past forty years are still worth only face value in the collector market; dealers will buy them at 10 to 20% *less* than face value!

I recommend that you sell these panes for face value if they are common varieties, or as near to face value as you can get. Then buy silver or play the racehorses if you enjoy gambling. If you hate to lose money, put it in the bank. If you seek an entertaining and informative hobby, with potential for long-range financial profits, try spending a portion of this pane money on rare and unusual stamps at your local stamp shop, and acquire a philatelic education in the process.

Money, after all, is only worth what the government says it is worth. Knowledge is priceless.

INVESTMENT STAMPS

So what are good stamps to buy, with an eye to future appreciation?

Those that already have good track records in the stamp marketplace. Well-centered, undamaged, mint or used stamps of these countries: United States, Canada, Great Britain, Japan, France, Germany (West for any issues, East for post-World War II issues of the 1940s and early 1950s), Switzerland, and former and present colonies of Great Britain. U.S. possessions like Hawaii, Guam, and Civil War-era Confederate States are also good stamps.

But not all issues of these places are prime investment material. Low press runs, high catalog value ($50 or more per stamp), extremely fine or superb centering in a stamp notorious for awful centering, multiples (blocks or strips still intact, as issued), and plate number blocks or marginal inscription blocks tend to be the better items for stamp investment. Catalog-listed errors, coil line pairs, proofs, and rare essays are often choice specialist material that will find an eager buyer even in a "down" market period.

How do stamps compare with other investments?

Salomon Brothers, the Wall Street investment analysis firm, has studied investments over the past fifteen years and has declared that rare postage stamps have outperformed stocks and bonds as an investment medium. The key word is *rare*. Common and cheap stamps have no collector demand and are a nightmare to sell.

How long are stamp price cycles?

The "booms" and "busts" vary, depending on the particular stamps, but in general, the whole stamp market saw its last peak in the winter of 1979-80, with some issues holding their values into 1981 and 1982. The crash of gold and silver, and the general countrywide economic recession of the early 1980s further depressed stamp values that were already overinflated (as hindsight shows!).

For example, the "Baby Zeppelin" 50-cent stamp of 1933 was selling for $250 in mint condition in 1980. It was readily available from dealers for $50 in the mid-1970s. Now you can pick up a nice copy, never hinged, for $100 retail.

The future can't be predicted with certainty, but many careful observers of the stamp market now believe that we are poised for a gradual upswing in rare stamp prices for the remainder of the 20th century.

OVERPAYING *How do you know if you're overpaying for a stamp?*

Shop around. Do you buy the first car you see or marry the first person who walks in the door? Check the prices of other dealers, study the auction catalogs, visit stamp shops and stamp shows, and only then consider sinking serious money into stamps. Some dealers have high overhead and high retail prices.

You will wait a long time to make a profit on stamps if you grossly overpay for them.

On the other hand, don't expect dirt cheap bargains. If the stamp seller is knowledgeable, the stamps won't come cheaply. Quality costs.

AIR MAILS

Are U.S. air mails good investments?

Yes. The first eighteen U.S. air mail stamps, from 1918 through 1933 have proven to be sound investments over the long term (ten to twenty years). Get them clean, undamaged, well-centered, and with rich color. The 6-cent orange of 1918, for example, tends to fade and discolor with time. Full gum if mint, lightly cancelled if used, and on cover or plate blocks are the best ways to invest in early U.S. air mails.

Shop around. Early U.S. air mails aren't unusually rare, they're just tremendously popular, and you may get a better deal (nicer stamp, cheaper price) if you shop a bit before buying. They're also easy to sell if you decide to liquidate; any dealer will buy them if they are in nice condition and worth maybe $100 or $200 retail.

FIRST-DAY COVERS

What is an average first-day cover worth?

Twenty-five cents, sometimes $1 or more if the cachet (envelope design on the left front side) is scarce. Common U.S. first-day covers of the last forty years can be found at any stamp show for twenty-five or fifty cents each. They probably cost the original owner more than that, so first-day covers are generally poor investments.

In the 1980s a third to a half million is a typical quantity for a U.S. commemorative first-day cover. There are not half a million stamp investors in the whole world, so how can common first-days be a good investment?

Of course, the rare first-day covers of sixty or more years ago sell for dozens or hundreds of dollars each, and these *are* desirable as investments.

I have noticed magazine advertisements selling U.S. first-day covers for $3.00 each. These are limited editions. Are these good investments?

No. Legitimate stamp dealers sell common first-day covers for less than $1 each. A few companies with high advertising budgets (and higher profit motives) sell overpriced covers in nonphilatelic magazines to beginning collectors and ignorant "investors" who haven't taken the time to learn about stamps. People who buy such junk are in for a rude awakening when they try to sell their supposed "heirloom rarities" to a stamp dealer who doesn't want them because he already has a couple of thousand in his stock.

A reputable business doesn't need a full-page ad to sell things that are rare and valuable. Good stamps and covers sell themselves. And the best investment I can think of is a trip to your neighborhood stamp shop to see for yourself what philatelic items are really worth.

You seem to have an aversion to U.S. first-day commemorative covers. What about the 2-cent reds of the 1920s? They sell for $20 to $30 each, as you must know. Two of my favorites are Washington praying at Valley Forge, issued May 26, 1928 at Norristown, PA, and the Sullivan Expedition issue of June 17, 1929, first-day city Perry, NY.

I started collecting covers at age ten when Mr. J.H. Wright, a lawyer acquaintance of my grandmother, sent me some U.S. first-day covers of that period. I later sold them to a local stamp dealer in my hometown of Joliet, Illinois for ten cents each when I needed a little pocket money. I currently specialize in collecting first-day covers related to California history, such as the Gold Rush issue of 1948 and the California Statehood Centennial stamp of 1950.

I'm not putting down first-day cover collecting. I'm just warning people that they are often poor investments. Anybody who comfortably spends $20 or $30 for one of the beautiful late 1920s "2-cent red" covers is probably a knowledgeable cover philatelist and doesn't need my first-day cover advice. I admire the 1920s covers, too!

COLUMBIANS AND TRANS-MISSISSIPPIANS

What is the current value of a complete set of U.S. Columbian Exposition stamps?

Maybe $10,000 mint, $5,000 used if in excellent condition. Beware of regummed and reperforated Columbians. Many have been altered and repaired since they were first issued in honor of the Chicago Columbian Exposition world's fair in 1893. The Columbians of 1893 and the Trans-Mississippian U.S. commemoratives of 1898 are prime investment stamps. They're notoriously off-center and with damaged gum for the unused ones. Well-centered examples with pristine gum bring double catalog value at auction.

PLATE BLOCKS

What do you think of plate blocks as investments?

Only if they are old, with no perforation separations, with nice gum (lightly hinged if disturbed), or catalog at least $50 each. A few plate blocks of U.S. stamps since 1950 are worth more than face value, but most aren't. For example, the $5 Hamilton plate block of four ($20 face value), issued in 1956, now sells at retail for $200 or more. Plate blocks of U.S. definitives of the 1920s or earlier, air mail plates before 1933, and U.S. commemorative plate blocks before 1920 tend to be good investments.

BE SUSPICIOUS OF TELEMARKETING

I received a telephone call offering to sell me investment-quality stamp heirlooms in limited editions. I became suspicious and hung up. Did I miss out on a good deal?

I don't buy anything over the telephone. Telemarketing has mushroomed into a billion dollar a year racket. If it is such a good deal, why do they have to beg strangers on the telephone to buy it? A tiny ad in any of the stamp magazines would bring serious buyers.

Heirloom, rare, limited, precious, valuable, and investment are words that some con artists like to use to get your attention. Everything is rare and limited in the sense that we don't have infinite quantities of it. And suppose it is truly *rare*. That doesn't necessarily mean that it is also in demand.

Legitimate stamp dealers don't push the idea of "investment" all the while they are talking to you. Ask yourself this question: If it is such a great investment, why don't they keep it themselves? Or draw their money out of the bank and buy up more of them for their own portfolios?

I only spend serious stamp money with established mail order stamp firms, long-running stamp auction houses, or at stamp stores that look like they've been around for a few years. If a stamp dealer advertises week after week in the stamp periodicals, he is probably okay. If he calls you on the telephone (and you have never heard of him) and pressures you to buy some great stamp "investments," he is probably a crook, or at least a very inefficient businessman.

GRAF ZEPPELINS   *What about the Graf Zeppelins as an investment? I know they're expensive, but they seem to be in heavy demand.*

The U.S. air mail set known as the Graf Zeppelins were first issued on April 19, 1930 and were withdrawn from sale on June 30, 1930. Sold in panes (sheets) of fifty stamps each, these ever-popular items had face values of: 65 cents (green), $1.30 (brown), and $2.60 (blue). That was a lot of money at the start of the Depression, and not many sets were sold.

In the summer of 1972, a Boston dealer wanted to sell me a set of Zeppelins for about $600, but I thought it was too much money and didn't buy it. In early 1980, the Zeppelins were inflated in market value along with many other stamps during the price boom at that time. In 1980, some Zeppelin sets changed hands for $8,000 for the three stamps in pristine mint condition.

That same choice set sells for $3,000 today at retail. $2,000 or less is the retail price of an off-center set or lightly-hinged copies.

So you see, stamps can go down in price as well as up. The Zeppelins are indeed popular, but they have been stagnating in value during the 1980s, and *may* be ready for some slow price appreciation in the next decade. No human can foretell the future, but I can think of worse stamps to buy for retention of value. If you are planning to be around in the year 2000, a choice set of Zepps could increase in value substantially if high rates of inflation come back.

NOTHING IS   *I keep seeing advertisements offering to sell rare stamps in*
GUARANTEED   *"investment portfolios" which are "guaranteed to rise in value at least 25% per year." This seems like a foolproof investment, but I have my doubts. How can I find out if these firms are ethical?*

Check with the local Better Business Bureau for the business history of the firm in question, and with the American Stamp Dealer's Association (ASDA), 3 School Street, Glen Cove, NY 11542. Also, write to the editors of stamp collecting publications and ask if they have heard of the companies.

Promises may be legal but not ethical. Some shady companies make fortunes by playing on the gullible public's greed, while technically staying entirely within the law.

What does "guaranteed to rise in value" mean? Will the company repay you your original purchase price for the stamps plus 25% per year interest if the stamps *don't* increase in price? Or is their fine-print guarantee merely limited to refunding the purchase price at any time you request it, even years later, in effect giving them an interest-free loan? Or will the company still be in business five years from now or will you be able to find their new name and location?

You can get a personal or car loan these days for 15% interest or less. If that stamp company was so sure that it had stamps that will increase 25% a year, then everybody who works for the company would take out a personal loan for as much money as they could get at 15% interest and buy their own company's stamps to earn the "guaranteed" 25%, resulting in a neat 10% profit for a little paperwork.

Sometimes shady companies even offer "certificates" of authenticity accompanying their merchandise, supposedly assuring the buyer that the stamps aren't counterfeit. But a certificate is only as reliable as the person who wrote it. And in the stamp investment world, counterfeit advice is much more common than counterfeit stamps.

QUANTITY AFFECTS PRICES

I took a group of embossed envelopes to a local dealer who appraised each envelope at $2, but quickly lowered the price to twenty-five cents each when he found out that I had about sixty of them. Is this fair? What good is an investment if it doesn't have a stable value?

When the dealer said "two dollars each," he might have been giving you a retail price appraisal. The twenty-five cents offer sounds like a wholesale buying price for material that he may not be especially interested in anyway.

Quantity has some influence on a dealer's buying prices. Common embossed envelopes (the envelopes with a stamp printed on them, as sold in post offices) are not easy to sell because they aren't rare or in great demand, so the dealer probably decided to offer you twenty-five cents apiece so that he could make a fair profit when he finally sells these envelopes one at a time to collectors at maybe seventy-five cents per envelope.

Don't assume that the dealer was dishonest; he was probably using sound business tactics. Suppose you took a nice pedigreed dog into a pet shop whose owner offered to pay $80 for it. What do you think this pet dealer would say if you then told him that you had twenty-five more dogs out in the car and wanted $80 each for them also?

Dealers buy stock that they feel they can sell in a reasonable amount of time. A neighborhood stamp shop that turns most of its stock over in a year is doing well. Remember this fact when you are investing in stamps: Buy what the dealers want to buy. And sell to a dealer who can absorb the quantities of each stamp that you want to sell.

HONEST DEALING

Whenever I go to a stamp dealer to sell stamps, they play a cat-and-mouse game with me. They usually say something like "What do you want for these stamps?" Then, if I name my price, they say, "Now what do you really want?" It seems to me that honest businesspeople should be upfront when buying or selling merchandise. I have concluded that stamp dealers are trying to take unfair advantage of collectors and investors by selling at top dollar and buying as cheaply as possible, regardless of the true worth of a collection.

I agree with you about dealers who play guessing games. Ethical and knowledgeable stamp dealers will not hesitate to put a buy (wholesale) or sell (retail) price on anything that they understand. Realize, of course, that over a half million major stamp varieties have been issued by the world's postal authorities, so no dealer can be a price expert on every stamp in existence!

Don't get discouraged when you meet a bad dealer. I've found that the stamp profession has better people than most other professions, and if a dealer can't talk prices with you in an intelligent and mature manner, walk away and find somebody who is more serious about doing business.

Where can I buy some cheap classics?

What do you mean by "cheap"? Ten percent off normal retail or auction price? Half price? Stamps with minor defects at a fraction of catalog value?

Defective stamps (known as "seconds"), such as those with missing corners or severe surface scrapes or pinholes, are hard to sell. Baseball cards and rare comic books are the only two other investment hobbies that I can think of where condition is of as much importance as it is in stamp collecting and investing. Quality sells and junk goes begging for an owner.

By all means, buy to fit your budget, but get one nice stamp for $50 rather than ten defective copies of the same issue for $5 each. I've never regretted buying an expensive stamp. I've often been disappointed when selling my cheap stamps because this fact is a basic rule of investment-grade collectibles: Cheap is often expensive in the long run.

Where should I store my stamp investments?

In a bank safe deposit box. Get one of sufficient size so that your album pages or stock cards can lie flat. And don't fill it up with junk; only expensive stamps should be locked up. No bank that I know of will insure the contents of its boxes, so get insurance for expensive items. Reasonable stamp insurance rates for collections stored in a bank or at home can be obtained from the American Philatelic Society. Write to: APS Insurance Plan, P.O. Box 157, Stevenson, MD 21153. Typical rates are around $100 premium for $30,000 liability coverage. This is the most popular stamp insurance category.

APPRAISALS   *How can I get my collection appraised?*

Any stamp dealer will give an appraisal. For valuable material, obtain an appraisal from the bigger dealers in town, listed with display ads in the Yellow Pages under "Stamps for Collectors." An expensive collection can be appraised for insurance or tax purposes, or for pre-sale estimates in investing liquidation strategy, but you must realize that the stamp dealer's time is worth something for a lengthy appraisal, and therefore a three hour appraisal job may run about 2 to 5% of the value of the collection. Some dealers will refund this fee if the collection is subsequently sold to them.

Also, tell the dealer which kind of appraisal you want: wholesale *value* (dealer buying price, or what you can expect to get if you sell it to him), retail *value* (dealer selling price, or what it might cost for you to replace the collection at current market values), or straight catalog *value* (which you can actually do yourself if you can identify the various stamps, and which may or may not accurately reflect current market prices).

PRICE ON REQUEST

What does P.O.R. mean? I sometime find this notation on price lists or in stamp auction catalogs.

P.O.R. means "Price on Request," indicating that the price is rather steep or fluctuating so much that by the time an ad is run, the actual selling price may change; or that the price, though high, is negotiable by mail or telephone; or that the seller wants only serious inquiries about the P.O.R. material, i.e., people who have the money to buy it. I haven't seen P.O.R. used in auction catalogs except in the sections of "private treaty" material offered for outright sale and listed at the back of the catalogs.

Chapter 12

Other Uses of Stamps

Donations to charities, use in artwork and crafts, prizes, use on personal mail, and as teaching tools in school classes — stamps certainly get around and may be used for things that their creators could hardly imagine!

Donations of philatelic material are gladly accepted by many charities and museums; beware, however, of fake "foundations" run by sharp operators who are looking for free valuable stamps. Check with local stamp dealers, stamp clubs, or the Internal Revenue Service to verify the non-profit status and legitimacy of a charity that asks for stamps.

STAMP DONATIONS *I want to donate some stamps and collecting materials to a non-profit organization. Do you have any suggestions?*

Many schools, churches, and youth groups with stamp clubs will be happy to receive your stamps and issue a receipt you can use for federal income tax deduction purposes. It is the responsibility of the donor to state the value of the stamps donated, and for large amounts there should be some kind of paper bill of sale or appraisal to support the taxpayer's claim.

Here is an organization that gladly accepts any kind of cancelled stamps, U.S. or foreign:

> Stamps for the Wounded
> 4201 Cathedral Avenue, N.W., #924E
> Washington, DC 20016

This 100 percent volunteer organization was founded in 1942 to distribute stamps to hospitalized military veterans to help occupy their lonely hours of rehabilitation. None of the workers has ever been paid a penny for services, and all donated stamps go directly to bedridden and convalescent patients who are veterans of our wars.

By sorting, soaking, and studying and mounting stamps for their albums, the joy of philately helps brighten the days for our former servicemen who received serious wounds in combat. Donations of stamps or cash are deductible for federal income tax purposes.

STAMPS AS DECORATION

I want to cover a wooden table's surface with stamps and coat them with a clear varnish or shellac, as a furniture decoration for my living room. Is this sensible?

I can just see every stamp collector cringing with fear at your suggestion. Stamps that are "painted over" with glue or varnish are likely to lose all of their collector's value forever because they are hard, if not impossible, to clean and restore to their original state. For similar reasons, you should never use transparent tape to cover stamps, or glue to affix them in a stamp album.

But, if you are certain that the stamps are extremely common and of little collector value (both of which can be disputed because occasionally minor or major varieties can be found in common mixtures), then you might ask for advice on a clear lacquer or varnish that won't dissolve paper. Check with a paint, crafts, art supply, or hardware store.

Remember, once a stamp is damaged, it is gone forever, so if you aren't sure of the value of the "table decoration" stamps, ask a dealer or philatelist to look at them *before* you start your project.

MIXTURES AS PRIZES

What kinds of stamps should we give away as prizes at our next charity fair?

Cheap ones, unless there is a raffle with a lot of money coming in from stamp collectors. Mixtures of cancelled U.S. and foreign stamps, first-day covers costing less than fifty cents each, and old album pages with stamps hinged on them make good prizes. If it is a non-profit organization, try to get stamp collectors (and dealers) to donate the stamp prizes; that way, the money raised will be pure profit.

The old time "mission mixtures" actually came from religious missionary organizations that accepted stamp donations which they sold to raise funds for their overseas missions. Today, many bulk stamp supply houses sell what they call "mission mixtures," but which in reality never saw the inside of a missionary's office. The whole point is that mission mixtures were supposedly unpicked and unsorted so that the buyer stood a slight chance of discovering some great rarity in them.

LIBRARY AND MUSEUM DONATIONS

Are stamps ever donated to museums? If so, what do they do with them after donation?

Some famous collections are partially on display (and the rest of the material is available for examination by researchers) in museums and other public locations. People do indeed donate their collections to museums, and a hotly debated topic is whether this is good or bad from a philatelic standpoint because many collectors claim that: (1) museums don't care about stamp collections; (2) only a tiny portion of a collection can be viewed and enjoyed at any given time by the general public; (3) the stamps are permanently removed from the market, so many philatelists are denied the opportunity of owning and studying them; and (4) the museum-displayed collection may be damaged by light, humidity, or dust accumulation in their permanent glass exhibition cases. In fact, the Smithsonian rotates its stamp displays and keeps strong light off of rare stamps and covers.

Still, there are public displays of stamps. Some of the better known ones are at the National Philatelic Museum of the Smithsonian Institution in Washington, DC; the Miller Collection of the New York Public Library; the Tapling Collection in the King's Library of the British Museum in London; the Cardinal Spellman Philatelic Museum in Weston, MA; and the philatelic collection at Boys Town near Omaha, NE.

If you plan to donate stamps or bequeath your collection to a museum or library, realize that they can sell or otherwise dispose of any or all of it at some future date, *regardless* of your original instructions. Thomas Jefferson said that the world belongs to the living because the dead are nothing and have no lasting rights; this is made quite evident in each generation's handling of its stamp collections.

COLLECTIBLE STAMPS ON MAIL

How can I brighten up my mail?

By using obsolete commemoratives as postage on the envelopes and packages that you send out. Most stamp shows and many stamp shops sell "postage" at face or near face value, i.e., stamps from the last forty years in mint condition that you can buy and use on your mail. There is a slight chance of it being stolen for the stamps, and when you use older stamps to frank a valuable parcel, be certain to insure or register it.

I even go as far as carefully selecting the theme of the stamps that I use on my mail. For example, medical commemoratives to doctors or hospitals, animals and "cartoon" designs to small children, and full plate blocks to stamp collectors or dealers. When you use old stamps in combinations to make up the current postal rate, your letter stands out in a person's mail and gets attention before it is opened!

STAMPS IN THE CLASSROOM

I am a school teacher. Can I use stamps in class?

If you're not already, your students are missing out on a fun and painless way to learn. Stamps show history, politics, science, and geography. I'm a teacher also, and I've often used U.S. commemorative stamps to teach my students about the history of flight, the famous medical topics (Red Cross, first doctors, "Help the Handicapped," etc.), and heroes from our past (Nathan Hale, the "four chaplains," and famous generals).

The key is to make it interesting when you use stamps in the classroom: don't give a lot of tests on them, and give a stamp to every student so they can put them in their notebooks and take them home for further study. Dealers and stamp shows sell common U.S. stamps in quantity. I like 3-centers because they're "old" and cheap to buy in bulk, and students will never have seen them before unless they're stamp collectors already.

Chapter 13

The Future of Stamp Collecting

The ever-increasing flood of new issues, the variable quality of stamp printing, how to get a stamp subject proposal considered by the Postal Service, the plague of forgeries, and future trends in stamp collecting over the next twenty years — all are included in this chapter, a bit speculative, of course, but based on my thirty-five years of collecting and observing the stamp hobby in its more obvious aspects.

The future! What a fantastic thought! And made all the more intriguing if stamps continue to have their magic place in the leisure hours of human lives.

NEW ISSUES   *Is the U.S. Postal Service issuing too many stamps? It seems that a collector on a tight budget has trouble keeping up with all of the new issues if he buys plate blocks, singles, and first-day covers of everything.*

Back when postage was three cents (even considering the effects of inflation since then), a 12-cent plate block of four stamps, plus a 3-cent single, plus a first-day cover costing maybe twenty-five cents or fifty cents to prepare — it was a lot easier to keep current with the dozen or so commemoratives that the Post Office Department (POD) issued annually.

It took a hundred years for the U.S. to issue 1,000 major varieties of definitive, commemorative, and air mail stamps put together, from 1847 through 1947. Since 1970 alone, another 1,000 major varieties of U.S. stamps have been released by the United States Postal Service (USPS); that's an average of fifty new stamps per year, with face values currently running twentyfive cents each for first class mail stamps.

And to make matters worse, a lot of the recent photogravure stamps are collected in margin blocks of twelve as a plate block. And first-day covers are more expensive to service, whether you prepare your own or subscribe to an automatic service. And definitives (regular issues) are being changed and replaced at a frightening rate, so any conservative collector should balk when staring at the $100 or more per year that it now costs to really get a comprehensive showing of new issues as singles, blocks, and covers.

MODERN PRINTING

What about the printing of modern U.S. stamps?

I think it is awful. Before the mid-1960s, most U.S. stamps were engraved; look at one under a magnifying glass and its intricate banknote-like ink lines become more beautiful. The current crop of U.S. photogravured stamps are ugly to the naked eye because of their fuzzy details and an indistinguishable confusion of color under magnification.

Great Britain makes passable artistic stamps with photogravure printing. We don't. So first of all, I'd like to see all U.S. stamps engraved. Then we should limit the number of new definitives flooding the post offices; we don't need new definitive designs every couple of years — the Presidentials of 1938 and the Liberty Series of 1954-68 lasted fifteen to twenty years each. And keep plate number blocks at four stamps each, and make souvenir sheets of low denominations so the collecting public isn't gouged every time souvenir sheets are issued.

Quality control should be increased. Too many U.S. stamps of the last quarter century have been found with major and minor printing errors. Printer's waste should go in the furnace, not out the door and into the albums of philatelists. U.S. stamps were once the envy of the world; let's make them so once again!

NEW STAMP SUBJECTS

I would like to get the Postal Service to issue a stamp in honor of my favorite sports hero. What is the procedure?

In the United States, all new stamp subject proposals go through this organization:

Citizens' Stamp Advisory Committee
c/o Stamp Development Branch
U.S. Postal Service
Washington, DC 20260

Write to them with details of your stamp suggestion. They welcome suggestions from private citizens for stamp ideas to honor famous (and not so famous!) people, animals, historical events or sites, sports, occupations (like nursing or teaching), and good causes (like "Fight Drug Abuse"). Impressive stationery and long petitions help, but it may take years for a proposal to be accepted by the Committee which consists of prominent citizens who debate the merits of proposed stamp designs, sending their recommendations to the Postmaster General who makes the final decision for new stamps.

The Committee receives a huge number of stamp proposals, including frivolous and bizarre ones, and they are forced to reject many worthy subjects simply because there are limits (!) on the number of stamps that the Postal Service will issue each year. Be courteous, be patient with your proposal, and if it is rejected all you've lost is some time and effort. For things like historical anniversaries, let them know a few years in advance, due to production time needed to prepare a stamp from scratch.

COLUMBIAN REISSUES   *Will the Columbians be reissued in 1992 or 1993?*

Some collectors are suggesting that the beautifully engraved set of sixteen values (from 1-cent to $5) of the U.S. Columbian stamps from 1893 be reissued in 1992 or 1993 to honor the 500th anniversary of the travels to America by Columbus. No reissuing decision has been made yet by the government.

Because the original set is worth thousands of dollars either mint or cancelled, the 1893 stamps might be somewhat "debased" by the easy availability of a similarly designed reissue version, a de facto stamp market devaluation in the opinion of many collectors.

Others suggest that a reissue could stimulate interest in the originals, thus *increasing* the desirability and market value of the 1893 stamps. Maybe issuing them in different colors or altered designs so that they could be readily distinguished from the originals.

On balance, I'm against reissuing them. As it stands now, if you want a Columbian, you either get the real thing or a counterfeit. If the USPS reissues the Columbians, even with altered colors or designs, then it seems to me that some collectors will be content with the 1993 versions at face value ($16.34). This would tend to decrease demand for the originals which aren't that rare to begin with (every auction has them); the 1893 stamps are expensive and worth investing in because of the tremendous demand for them (which might be partly satisfied with future reprints).

FUTURE COLLECTING TRENDS

What do you see as trends in stamp collecting in the immediate future? What will be the popular stamps for the next twenty years?

If any person could actually foresee the future, they would be powerful and rich beyond anyone's wildest dreams. The casinos of Las Vegas and every local racetrack operate on a law of nature that states that human beings cannot foresee the future with certainty. Still, we can take an intelligent look at what the future might bring in stamp collecting and philatelic investing:

(1) Further specialization will be the norm in the 1990s and early 21st century. With well over half a million major varieties of stamps in the catalog listings, no collector can hope to acquire more than the majority of the common ones with a moderate budget over a lifetime. I see more country specialization, albums for France or Israel (for example) being more popular than worldwide albums. Topical collecting, omnibus issues, limited time periods (with more emphasis on the 20th century as 19th century stamp prices shoot through the roof), and single stamp categories (like air mails of Asia) will be the rule rather than the collecting exception for most philatelists.

(2) Lightly hinged (LH) stamps will ever so slowly start increasing in acceptability among collectors because never hinged (NH) examples will become more scarce and expensive. With the current epidemic of regumming going on, I don't see why an intelligent collector insists on paying double or triple for a stamp that supposedly has original gum (OG) when compared with a stamp that is lightly hinged. NH merits a premium but not 200%. Or to look at it realistically, would you rather have three stamp collections LH, or one stamp collection with NH for the same amount of money invested?

(3) Covers will continue to boom in popularity. Neglected during the first third of this century, and semi-frowned upon by ultra-conservative stamp exhibitors who believe that true philately is stamps, not envelopes, the collecting and study of covers (postal history) will occupy the time and attention of numerous collec-

tors over the next twenty years. Covers tell a story, you get a big item for your money, and they are for sale in quantities and quality to suit any budget (twenty cents to $20,000 or more per cover, literally!).

(4) More expensive collecting tools will be an unfortunate trend in philately as time goes on. Already the standard catalogs and worldwide albums are broken up into separate volumes, and the several thousand new issues per year from the world's stamp-producing authorities won't decrease the number of stamps on the market. Gone are the ten-cent packets of hinges or $1 sacks of mission mixtures. Plastic mounts and hingeless albums are very expensive and increase the cost of collecting mint stamps.

Beginners won't have a whole selection of stamp tongs, magnifiers, and perforation gauges in their desk drawers. I predict fewer but more expensive (even adjusted for inflation) collecting tools in the average stamp collector's hobby room.

(5) Back-of-the-book (BOB) stamps will definitely see more attention and investor dollars in the next quarter century. Already the Hunting Permit Stamps (Ducks), Match and Medicine revenues, U.S. possessions (Guam and Hawaii), and Parcel Posts/Special Deliveries type of material has seen a price boom since 1970. Expect sharp philatelists to scour the standard catalogs, searching for "sleepers" that could be the next hot item in the stamp market. As early definitives and pre-1920 U.S. commemoratives escalate in price, many newer collectors may be attracted by the wonderful variety and historical significance of back-of-the-book stamps.

(6) U.S. plate block collecting will continue to stagnate, a victim of the foolish production of photogravure blocks of twelve which effectively killed, for many collectors, the yearly interest in getting all the new plate blocks at the post office; and higher face value plate blocks discourage collectors on a lower budget.

FUTURE FORGERIES   *Will stamp forgeries and counterfeits exist in the future?*

As long as they continue to reward their crooked makers with handsome profits for a lot of work.

I recommend getting any expensive stamp expertized if you have *any* doubt as to its authenticity. Fees range from $10 up, but it may be worth it to verify the genuineness of a rare stamp.

These are the two largest expertizing organizations in the United States. Write to them for a list of their fees, enclosing a self-addressed stamped envelope.

American Philatelic Expertizing Service
P.O. Box 8000
State College, PA 16803

Philatelic Foundation
21 East 40th Street
New York, NY 10016

Bibliography

These are some of the best stamp books ever written. Included are easy-to-read postal history and philatelic guidebooks as well as highly technical classics by the most famous research philatelists in American history. Many are out of print, but can be supplied by stamp literature dealers like: Leonard H. Hartmann, P.O. Box 36006, Louisville, KY 40233. Mr. Hartmann carries a comprehensive stock of stamp books, services want lists for anything that he doesn't have at the moment, and buys stamp books that he needs for his business. Of course, I have done business with him but have no financial interest in his company.

Ashbrook, Stanley B. *The United States One Cent Stamp of 1851-1857.* Harry L. Lindquist, New York, 1938. In two volumes, a brilliant in-depth study of the pre-Civil War 1-cent stamp. Sets the standard by which all other technical books are judged in philately.

Brazer, Clarence W. *Essays for United States Adhesive Postage Stamps.* Quarterman Publications, Lawrence, MA, 1977 reprint. The "bible" of U.S. stamp essays — designs that were proposed but never used for U.S. stamps.

Brookman, Lester G. *The United States Postage Stamps of the Nineteenth Century.* Harry L. Lindquist, New York, 1967. Originally published in two volumes, this three-volume classic describes in detail the 19th century U.S. stamps from Brookman's personal observations. Out of print, the 1967 edition sells for several hundred dollars per set. Brookman is often quoted.

Chase, Carroll, Dr. *The Three Cent Stamp of the United States, 1851-1857 Issue.* Quarterman Publications, Lawrence, MA, 1976 reprint. Technical writing by a serious philatelic scholar who devoted a lot of time in the study of one stamp issue.

Dietz, August. *The Postal Service of the Confederate States of America.* The Dietz Press, Richmond, VA, 1929. And by the same author: *Confederate States Catalog and Handbook.* Dietz Publishing Co., Richmond, VA, 1959. The classic works giving the background of Confederate mail service.

Johl, Max G. and King, Beverly S. *The United States Postage Stamps of the Twentieth Century.* Originally published in four volumes in the 1930s, the 1976 reprint by Quarterman Publications, Lawrence, MA covers the regular issues that were described in the original work. The standard reference on U.S. stamps of this century.

Herst, Herman, Jr. *Nassau Street* (1960) and *Fun and Profit in Stamp Collecting.* Duell, Sloan and Pearce, New York, 1962. Entertaining reading about stamp dealing in New York City, with timeless advice from probably the best philatelic writer. Anyone who doesn't enjoy reading Mr. Herst's writings either isn't human or isn't a stamp collector! Reprints of these books are currently available in softcover for $9.95 and $7.95 respectively (postpaid) from: *Linn's Stamp News*, P.O. Box 29, Sidney, OH 45365.

Kehr, Ernest A. *The Romance of Stamp Collecting.* Thomas Y. Crowell Co., New York, 1947, 1956. Written by the former stamp news editor of the *New York Herald Tribune*, this book makes good late night reading, with 352 pages covering the history of stamp collecting, including personal conversations that he had with Franklin Roosevelt regarding the President's well-known interest in stamps.

Loso, Foster W. (editor). *The Stamp Collectors' Round Table.* Frederick A. Stokes Co., New York, 1937. 360 pages of precious non-technical easy-to-read essays written by so many of the philatelic greats of the 1930s, including Rich, Johl, Dietz, Perry, Ashbrook, and Brazer. Out of print, but in many public libraries like the Santa Monica, CA library where I just found the original 1937 edition sitting on the circulating shelves!

Luff, John N. *Postage Stamps of the United States.* Scott Stamp and Coin Co., New York, 1902. Was the basic U.S. stamp reference before Brookman's work. Out of print, but can still be bought from philatelic literature dealers for less than $100.

Mueller, Barbara R. *United States Postage Stamps — How to Collect, Understand, and Enjoy Them.* D. Van Nostrand Co.,

Princeton, NJ, 1958. Well-organized, well-printed summary of U.S. stamp issues, from the first in the 1840s up through modern commemoratives and special use stamps. Many black-and-white photos of stamps and covers.

Planty, Earl. *United States First Day Cover Catalog of Classic Cachets, 1923-1933.* Earl Planty, Coral Springs, FL, 1974. One of the first authors to explain the different cachet (envelope) designs of first-day covers.

Scheele, Carl H. *A Short History of the Mail Service.* Smithsonian Institution Press, Washington, DC, 1970. An excellent history of mail service, from ancient times to today, with emphasis on postal service in America from Colonial days to the present. Lots of facts, well organized, a wealth of information. At the time of publication, Scheele was Associate Curator in Charge of Philately at the Smithsonian.

Sloane, George B. *Sloane's Columns.* Bureau Issues Association, West Somerville, MA, 1961. Reprinted in 1980, but the original has better quality printing. A collection of the columns Sloane wrote for *Stamps* magazine over almost thirty years. Covers classics and back-of-the-book U.S. stamps. Both editions are available for around $50 each.

Thorp, Prescott H. *The Thorp-Bartels Catalogue of United States Stamped Envelopes.* 1954 Century Edition, two-volume reprint in 1968 by Prescott Thorp, Netcong, NJ. The standard reference for U.S. stamped envelopes (embossed postal stationery).

Tiffany, John K. *The History of the Postage Stamps of the United States.* C.H. Mekeel, St. Louis, 1886-87. A 19th century U.S. stamp reference, available for less than $100 on the used book market today.

Turner, George and Thomas Stanton. *Pat Paragraphs.* The complied writings of U.S. classics philatelic scholar Elliott Perry, derived from fifty-eight booklets by Perry. 648 pages in the 1981 printing, this reference sells for around $50.

Walcott, George. *The George Walcott Collection of Used Civil War Patriotic Covers.* Compiled by Robert Laurence of New York in 1934, the 1974-75 printing by Robert W. Grant, Hanover, MA is freely available from literature dealers. Lists over 3,000 envelope cachet designs of Civil War patriotics.

Williams, L.N. and M. *Fundamentals of Philately*. American Philatelic Society, State College, PA, 1971. In their preface to this 629-page hardcover book, the authors state that this reference is intended mainly for "adult beginners." When you're done reading it, you'll no longer be a beginner because this book explains in great detail how stamps are manufactured. Profusely illustrated with black-and-white photos and drawings. In many large public libraries and available from literature dealers.

Glossary

This is a glossary of the most common stamp terms and their recognized abbreviations as used in the standard catalogs, dealer price lists, auction descriptions, and at stamp exhibitions.

ADHESIVE: A postage stamp, with or without its original gum.

AMERICAN PHILATELIC SOCIETY (APS): Largest stamp collector organization in the United States. Issues expertizing certificates.

AMERICAN STAMP DEALER'S ASSOCIATION (ASDA): The largest and best known stamp dealer's organization in the United States. Being an ASDA member helps verify a dealer's integrity.

APPROVALS: Stamps sent by mail from companies to collectors who choose the ones they wish to keep, and return the balance with their payment for items retained.

AS IS: A sales term meaning that the lot cannot be returned for a refund once it is bought and taken home. Usually refers to defective stamps.

AVERAGE (AV or AVE or AVG): Lower grade stamps, generally not of investment or exhibition quality.

BACK OF BOOK (BOB): Section of the standard catalog after the regular issues and commemoratives. Includes special deliveries, postage dues, revenues, etc.

BACKSTAMPED (B/S): Handstamped postal marking on the back of a cover.

BISECT: Stamp cut in half and cancelled on a cover. Used to pay half the postage value of the original uncut stamp.

BLIND PERF: Perforation holes not punched out, but impressions of the hole puncher are evident. Not imperforate or of the market value of true imperforates.

BLOCK (BLK or ⊞ or ☐) : Four or more stamps still joined together in block form. Unless stated otherwise, refers to block-of-four.

BOURSE: Place where dealers meet to buy and sell stamps to the public. Also called a stamp show.

BRITISH NORTH AMERICA (BNA): Stamps of Canada and its former independent stamp-issuing provinces.

BRITISH PHILATELIC ASSOCIATION (BPA): Great Britain stamp society. Issues expertizing certificates.

BULL'S EYE: Cancel which is centered more or less wholly on a stamp. Also called "socked-on-the-nose" (SOTN or SON).

CACHET: A printed design on the left front of a cover, placed there for philatelic purposes; often a first day cover.

CANCELLED TO ORDER (CTO): Stamps which never saw postal use, but instead are mass cancelled in full panes by a country interested in selling them at a discount to collectors for revenue.

CATALOG VALUE (CV or C/V or CAT VAL): Price quote for a stamp in a standard philatelic catalog.

CENSORED: Cover which has been handstamped to indicate that it has been read by a censor; usually military mail.

CENTERING: How well a stamp's design is centered relative to the unprinted margin between the design and perforations or stamp's edge. Off center stamps are so described, for example, centered to top (CTT) or centered to bottom (CTB).

CHANGELING: A stamp whose color has been chemically changed since it left the post office where it was sold.

CINDERELLA: A paper label which is not a postage stamp, although it often appears to be. Not necessarily meant to defraud; may be a fantasy issue of a nonexistent country or a privately-produced adhesive for business purposes, etc.

CIRCULAR DATE STAMP (CDS): A circular cancel which has the date appearing inside.

CLASSIC: A stamp issued over a century ago. Old, rare, and valuable stamps.

COIL: Stamps issued in roll form, with two opposite edges being straight.

COLLATERAL: Material related to stamps, such as route maps, Postmaster General autographs, post office photos, etc. Often used to enhance a philatelic exhibit.

COLOR SHIFT: Misalignment of colors, a production error on a multicolored stamp.

COMMEMORATIVE (COMMEM): A stamp issued for a limited time period to honor a person, place, or thing. Not a regular or definitive issue.

CORNER CARD: Return address portion of an envelope; often referring to that area on nineteenth century covers.

COVER (CVR or ⊠): An envelope designed for postal use.

CREASE (CR): A permanent fold on a stamp or cover. Mentioned in auction descriptions as a warning because creases lower a stamp's value.

CUT CANCEL (CC): A cancellation which cuts through the stamp. Usually drastically reduces the value.

CUT SQUARE: The printed stamp area of an embossed envelope, cut away from the rest of the cover.

CUT TO SHAPE (CTS): A stamp, usually imperforate, which has had its margins cut to border the printed design. Usually reduces the value when compared with one not cut to shape.

DEAD COUNTRY: A nonexistent nation or political entity which once issued its own stamps but no longer does.

DEFINITIVE: Regular postal issue, on sale for a long time at post offices. Not a commemorative.

DISTURBED GUM (DG): Damaged stamp gum.

ENTIRE: Full piece of postal stationery (as opposed to a cut square).

ERROR, FREAK, ODDITY (EFO): Category of stamps which are errors.

ESSAY (E): A proposed stamp design, often in stamp form. Should not be the finally accepted design or it would then be known as a proof.

ESTIMATED (EST): Estimated net value, a predicted auction price.

EX: An auction term meaning from a famous collection; for example, EX-Ashbrook. Gives a philatelic item more prestige and possibly more value due to its provenance.

EXPLODED: A post office booklet of stamps which has been broken apart into its component panes, covers, etc.

EXTREMELY FINE (EF or XF): A stamp grade meaning high quality; just below the grade of Superb.

FAULTS (FLTS): With damage.

FIELD POST OFFICE (FPO): A military postal facility in the theater of conflict. Could also be an army post office (APO).

FINE (F): A stamp grade meaning minimally acceptable quality, above Very Good but below Very Fine. Perforations usually clear of the design.

FIRST DAY COVER (FDC): An envelope with a stamp cancelled on its first day of issue.

FIRST FLIGHT COVER (FFC): An envelope flown on the first day of an air mail route.

FISCAL: Revenue use of a stamp; often pen cancelled, usually reducing its value from non-fiscal or regular postal use.

FOLDED LETTER (FL): A letter folded and sent without an envelope.

FRAME: The printed border of a stamp's design, between the vignette in the center and the edge of the stamp's paper.

FRANKED: The postage used to pay a letter; for example, franked with two stamps. Free franks have no stamps attached.

FRONT: The stamped and addressed side of a cover; when used alone it refers to just the front of an envelope remaining. Usually reduces the value compared to a full intact envelope.

FUGITIVE INK: Ink used in stamp printing that dissolves in water.

GRILL: Little impressions in stamp paper to let the cancel's ink soak in to prevent reuse of the stamp. Prevalent on certain nineteenth century U.S. stamps.

GUM: The adhesive glue on the back of a stamp.

GUTTER PAIR (G/PR): Two stamps separated by a piece of unprinted paper, as a result of production processes.

HANDSTAMPED (HS or H/S): Cancelled with a handstamping device.

HEAVILY CANCELLED (HC): Abnormally dense cancel ink on a stamp; greatly reduces a used stamp's value.

HEAVILY HINGED (HH): A stamp with hinge paper adhering in distracting amounts. Reduces value from lightly hinged.

HIGHWAY POST OFFICE (HPO): A mobile post office located in a truck.

HINGED (H): Showing evidence of having been hinged (as opposed to mint, never hinged).

HINGE REMNANTS (HR): Pieces of hinge adhering to a stamp.

IMPERFORATE (IMPERF): Stamps issued without perforations.

INVERTED (INVT): Error in which part of a stamp's design appears abnormally upside down.

LEFT, RIGHT (L, R): Auction descriptions used in abbreviations: CTL (centered to left).

LIGHTLY CANCELLED (LC): Pleasingly light cancel on a stamp; usually enhances its value.

LIGHTLY HINGED (LH): Just a trace of gum disturbance where a hinge once was on a stamp.

LINE PAIR (LP or L/P): A guideline copy of a pair of adjacent coil stamps. Used to help guarantee the coil nature of the stamps.

LOCAL: Limited geographical use, such as stamps made for use in one city.

LOWER LEFT/LOWER RIGHT (LL/LR): Positions on single stamps or blocks.

MANUSCRIPT (MS): Another name for pen cancellation.

MARGIN (MRGN): The unprinted area between the outside of a stamp's design and the edge of the paper.

MARGINAL INSCRIPTION (MI): Printed information in the attached selvage around a stamp.

MINOR DEFECT (MD): Small damaged area of a stamp. Beware of advertised minor defects turning out to be major when they are purchased!

MINT (M or *): An unused stamp with gum if issued as such.

MINT, NEVER HINGED (MNH or **): The gum on a stamp is undisturbed by hinging or other means.

MISPERFORATED (MISPERF): Perforations out of alignment instead of being in their usual place between stamp designs.

MULTIPLE: More than one of the same stamp still attached to each other as issued (with or without perforations).

NEVER HINGED (NH or **): Gum which shows no evidence of ever having been hinged.

NO GUM (NG): A stamp without any gum on the back, usually referring to one which once had gum. Another name for a no gum stamp is *unused* (as opposed to *mint* which means with gum).

OBSOLETE: Stamps which are no longer for sale in post offices.

OFF CENTER: A stamp whose design is significantly not centered on the paper.

OFF PAPER: Used stamps which have been soaked off of or otherwise removed from their envelopes.

ORIGINAL GUM (OG): The gum as issued is still on the back of a stamp. May or may not be hinged. If original gum, never hinged, it is designated OGNH.

OVERPRINT (OVPT): Official inked impression that has been added to a stamp's design after it was first printed. Overprints may be words or face value changes.

PAIR (PR): Two adjacent stamps still joined together as issued.

PANE: What non-philatelists call a "sheet," the form in which stamps are sold in the post office; the largest flat connected group of stamps that a postal patron can buy.

PERFORATED INITIALS (PERFINS or PI's): Little holes in the configuration of alphabet letters which are punched into stamps as a security, anti-theft measure. Used by businesses and stamp-issuing governments.

PERFORATION (PERF): One of the holes punched between stamps to facilitate separation.

PHILATELIC FOUNDATION CERTIFICATE (PFC): An expertizing document that accompanies stamps certified as genuine by the prestigious Philatelic Foundation of New York City.

PHILATELIC TRADER'S SOCIETY (PTS): A London-based organization of worldwide stamp dealers. A PTS logo displayed in a dealer's ad helps verify his integrity.

PHILATELIC USE: A cover which was prepared and mailed by a philatelist. Also called *controlled mail*. The opposite of unplanned commercial mail.

PHILATELY: Stamp collecting. Literally, "love of exemption from taxation" from the Greek words *philos* (love) and *ateleia* (exempt from tax), referring to postage being prepaid by a stamp. Technically, philately means the serious study of stamps, not just accumulating them.

PLATE BLOCK (PB): A number or inscription block, usually of four stamps. Also called plate number block (PNB).

PLATE NUMBER (PL NO or PL #): The control production number imprinted on the selvage attached to a stamp.

POST CARD (PC or P/C): A picture card sold to tourists for mailing. Don't confuse with *postal card*.

POSTAGE DUE (PD): Mail sent without enough postage. Also refers to special stamps issued to collect insufficient postage on undelivered mail.

POSTAL CARD (PC or P/C also): A government-issued card that you buy at a post office, blank on the back, and printed with a stamp on the front upper right-hand corner.

POSTAL HISTORY: The study of mail service. Also refers to covers as a synonym.

POSTAL STATIONERY: Embossed stamped envelopes and postal cards.

POSTMARK (PMK): A marking on mail to indicate date mailed, routes travelled, amount of postage paid, etc. May be stamped with a preformed device or handwritten.

POST OFFICE DEPARTMENT (POD): What the U.S. Postal Service was called prior to 1971.

PRECANCEL (PREC): A stamp that has been cancelled prior to being stuck on a piece of mail.

PROOF (P or PR or PRF): A trial impression of a stamp in its design as finally issued, either in black ink or in the color of issues. Don't confuse with essays.

RAILWAY POST OFFICE (RPO): A postal station on board a railway car.

REGUMMED (RG): An unused stamp that has had faked gum applied after its original gum washed off.

REPRINT (R): A stamp made from the original equipment long after the first issue of it became obsolete.

ROULETTE (R): A method of separating stamps by slits in the paper instead of perforations.

SCOTT CATALOG VALUE (SCV): The price of a stamp quoted in the official Scott Catalog.

SELVAGE (SEL or SELV): The paper (either printed or blank) that is attached outside of the stamps on a pane. Also spelled selvege or selvedge.

SEMI-POSTAL: A stamp issued for a charity purpose, with two values imprinted on it; one for payment of postage and one for donation to charity. Listed under "B" numbers in the Scott catalogs.

SEPARATION (SEP): Stamps separated (usually partially) at their natural perforations.

SET: A complete group of stamps of similar designs, as issued. Designated by catalog numbers like: 75-83; as opposed to an incomplete set with some stamps missing, shown by a diagonal line between the end values: 75/83.

SE-TENANT: Stamps of different designs attached adjacently to each other as issued.

SHEET: The complete piece of paper of stamps as originally printed. Often broken into two or four panes for post office sale. When non-philatelists say they bought a *sheet* of post office stamps, they really mean that they bought a *pane*.

SHORT PERFORATION (SH PF): A perforation "tooth" pulled off of a stamp.

SLEEPER: A stamp that is undervalued in the catalogs or marketplace. Unrecognized underpriced items.

SOUVENIR SHEET (SS or S/S): A small pane of one or more stamps, issued for commemorative purposes by a postal government, often specifically for collectors.

SPACE FILLER: A badly damaged, expensive stamp that takes the place of the extremely valuable, sound copy which the collector cannot afford.

SPECIMEN (S): A stamp overprinted with a number or the word "Specimen" for distribution to governments or other authorities to serve as a sample of a newly-issued stamp.

STAMPLESS COVER: An envelope that went through the mails without adhesive stamps on it. Usually refers to pre-Civil War mail before adhesive stamps became widespread.

STRAIGHT EDGE (SE or S/E): A stamp with a natural or cut straight edge, although originally issued as perforated in most cases.

SUPERB (SUP or S): The top grade for stamps. Essentially perfectly centered with no defects. Used recklessly by liberal graders; very few old stamps are technically superb.

SURCHARGE: An overprint on a stamp that changes its face value.

TEAR (TR): A rip in a stamp. Used as an auction description. Enormously decreases a stamp's value in most cases.

TETE-BECHE: Adjacent stamps from the same pane where one design is upside down in relation to the other.

THIN (TH): A thinned area of a stamp; reduces its value.

TIED ON: A stamp on a cover with the cancel covering both the stamp and cover's paper; helps to insure that the stamp was in fact used on that cover.

TIED TO PIECE (TTP or ▲): A stamp cancelled on a small piece of the original envelope, with the cancel tying on the stamp.

TINY (T): An auction description, for example, tiny thin (TTH), tiny crease (TCR).

TOP/BOTTOM (T/B): Auction description, for example, a top block: T ⊞ . Refers to positions.

TOPICALS: Stamps picturing a certain subject, like animals, sports, airplanes. Also called *thematics*.

UNITED STATES POSTAL SERVICE (USPS): Our present postal service, so-called since 1971 when it replaced the old Post Office Department.

UNLISTED (UNL): Not listed in the standard catalogs.

UNUSED (UN): Never cancelled. Technically a stamp that has never been cancelled, but has also lost its original gum. Used as a sloppy definition for mint sometimes.

UPPER LEFT/UPPER RIGHT (UL/UR): Positions on single stamps or blocks.

USED (U or ⊙ or ●): A cancelled stamp.

VARIETY (VAR): A subtype of a basic catalog numbered stamp. For example, color or perforation varieties.

VERY FINE (VF): A high grade stamp, better than fine but less nice than extremely fine. Very fine stamps are usually great for discriminating collectors and investors.

VERY GOOD (VG): An inferior stamp grade, below fine. Very good stamps usually have damaged perforations or the design is cut by the perforations.

VERY LIGHTLY HINGED (VLH): The most delicately imaginable evidence of a trace of gum disturbance where a hinge once was.

VIGNETTE: The main picture or central design of a stamp.

WALLPAPER: A derogatory term meaning unnecessary stamps sold by unscrupulous governments to get money from collectors. Synonymous with sand dunes, black blot, or Communist bloc issues.

WATERMARK (WMK): A slightly thinned area of a stamp that is impressed on it at the time of manufacture of the stamp's paper, as a security measure against counterfeiting.

WITH/WITHOUT (W and W/O): Auction abbreviations. For example, without gum: W/O G.

Index

A

Adhesive, 135
Ads, classified and display, 26-7
Advertising covers, 50
Air mail stamps, 30, 112
    as investments, 112
Air mails, 64
American Lung Association, 35
American National Red Cross, 35
American Philatelic Expertizing
    Service, 130
American Philatelic Society, 12,
    24, 27, 78, 100, 118, 135
American Stamp Dealers Associ-
    ation, 100, 115, 135
*American Stampless Cover Cata-
    log*, 52
American Topical Association, 34
Antique shops, 19
Appraisals, 118-9
    typical cost of, 118
Approvals, 135
Artcraft Covers, 48
Artmaster, 48
As is, 135
Ashbrook, Stanley B., 131
Auctions, 19, 20-3, 26
    bidding at, 21-3
    buying stamps at, 19, 20-2
    by mail, 21-3
Australian "Roos", 80
"Autograph letter signed" (ALS),
    52
Average (AV or AVE or AVG),
    135

B

Back of book (BOB), 135
Backstamped (B/S), 135
Balloon covers, 41, 45-6

Baruch, Bernard, 106
Beginners' collections, 15
Better Business Bureau, 115
Bibliography, 131-4
"Bid boards", 20
Bisect, 135
Blazer, Clarence W., 131
Blind perforations, 97, 136
Blocks, 30, 136
Bluenose, 81
Bourse, 24, 136
    stamp, 24
Brightening up your mail with
    obsolete commemoratives,
    123-4
British Commonwealth special-
    ties, 87
British North America (BNA),
    136
British Philatelic Association
    (BPA), 136
Brookman, Lester G., 131
Bull's Eye, 136
Bureau of Engraving and Print-
    ing, 36, 100

C

Cachet, 136
Canada, early stamps, 80-1
Canal Zone stamps, 69-70
Cancel date errors, 102-3
Cancelled stamps, 30
Cancelled to order (CTO), 136
Cancels, 36, 48, 51
    rare, 51
    special, 48
Cancels and covers, 41-52
Catalog prices, 109
Catalog value (CV or C/V or
    CAT VAL), 136

Catalog values, 108-9
Categories of stamps, 29-40
Censored, 136
Centering, 136
Changeling, 136
Chase, Dr. Carroll, 131
Christie's Stamp Department, 21
Christmas seals, 35
Cinderella, 136
Circular date stamp (CDS), 136
Citizens' Stamp Advisory Com-
    mittee, 126
Civil War Postage Currency, 71-2
Classic, 137
Classified ads, 26-7
    honest, 26
Classified ads buying or selling
    stamps, 27
Cleaning and protecting
    philatelic items, 93-4
Cleaning and repairing, ethics of,
    89
Clubs, stamp collectors, 15-6
Coil, 137
Collateral, 137
*Collecting Stamps for Pleasure
    and Profit*, 9
Collecting stamps, 11-3, 66-8
    cost of, 12
    reasons for, 13
    specialized, 66-8
    why people start, 11
Collecting trends of the future,
    128-9
Collections, 15, 16, 85-6
    for beginners, 15
    never finished, 16
    worldwide, 85-6
Collectors, as investors, 106
Color errors, 101

Color shift, 137
Columbian reissues, 127-8
Columbians, 61-3
Commemorative (COMMEM), 137
Commemoratives, 31-3, 123-4
   obsolete, using to brighten up your mail, 123-4
Commemoratives or definitives, which better to collect, 31-3
Commercial covers, 41-2
Condition, 95, 107-8
   definitions of, 95
   effect on market value, 107-8
Confederate States Catalog and Handbook, 132
Confederate States Postmasters' Provisionals, 75-6
Corner Card, 137
Cost of collecting stamps, 12
Covers, 41-52, 137
   advertising, 50
   balloon, 41, 45-6
   commercial, 41-2
   definition, 41
   expedition, 47
   first-day, 41, 47-8
   Gold Rush, 43
   inaugural, 52
   military, 41, 43-5
      prices, 45
   philatelic, 41-2
   Pony Express, 41
   space, 41, 50-1
   stampless, 51-2
Covers and cancels, 41-52
Crease (CR), 137
Creases, 89-90
   effect on market value, 90
Cut cancel (CC), 137
Cut square, 137
Cut to shape (CTS), 137

D

Damages and defects, 89-95
Danish Stamps, 85
Dead country, 137
   definition of, 81-2

Dealers, 24-6. 100, 116-7
   crooked, 24-6, 100, 116-7
   ethical, 26
   ethical and otherwise, 117
   quantity effect on prices offered, 116-7
   specializing in errors, 100
   stamp, 24-6
Defects, effect on value, 94-5
Defects and damage, 89-95
   creases, 89-90
   damaged perforations, 92
   disturbed gum, 89, 91-2
   pinholes, 89, 90-1
   stains, 89-90
Definitives, 31-3, 137
Deltiology, 34
Demonitized stamps, 68-9
Dietz, August, 132
Disturbed gum (DG), 137
   as defect, 89, 91-2
Domestic Mail Manual (Postal Service), 48
"Duck" stamps, 37-8, 65
Dumaine, Bob, 65

E

1847 issues, 75
Earl P. L. Apfelbaum, Inc.
Encased postage stamps, 77-8
Entire, 137
Envelopes, glassine, 59
Error, freak, oddity (EFO), 137
Errors, 97-104
   5-cent color, 100-101
   blind perforations, 97
   cancel date, 102-3
   color, 101
   dealers specializing in, 100
   imperforate, 99
   mis-registered colors, 103
   plate smears, 99
   postal cards, 102
   price of, 99
   watermark, 103-4
Errors, Freaks, and Oddities Collectors Club, 97
Essay (E), 138

Essays for United States Adhesive Postage Stamps, 131
Estimated (EST), 138
Ethics of stamp repairs, 89, 94
EX, 138
Expedition covers, 47
Expertizing certificate, 101
Expertizing organizations, 129-130
Exploded, 138
Extremely fine (EF or XF), 138

F

5-cent color error, 100-101
$5 definitives, 73-4
Fakes, 101
Fakes, regummed, 92
Falkland Islands stamps, 86
Faults, (FLTS), 138
Field Post Office (FPO), 138
Finds, rare, 23-4
Fine (F), 138
First day cover (FDC), 138
First flight cover (FFC), 138
First-day covers, 41, 47-8
   as investments, 112-3
Fiscal, 138
Folded letter (FL), 138
Foreign stamps, 79-87
   inexpensive beginner kits, 79
Forgeries, 51, 125
Frame, 138
Franked, 138
Fraud, 77-8
Front, 138
"Fugitive ink", 53, 138
Fun and Profit in Stamp Collecting, 132
Fundamentals of Philately, 133
Future of stamp collecting, 125-130
Future trends, 128-130
   catalogs and collecting tools, 129
   collecting, 128
   forgeries and counterfeits, 129-130
   plate blocks, 129

G

"Garbage Card", 102
George Walcott Collection of Used Civil War Patriotic Covers, The, 133
German cancels (rare), 84
Germs on stamps, 58
Glassine envelopes, 59
Glossary, 135-145
Gobie, Henry M., 65
Gold Medal Mail Sales, 21
Gold Rush covers, 43
Government saving stamps, 38
Graf Zeppelins, 74
    as investment, 115
Great Britain, early stamps, 79-80
Grill, 139
Gum, 139
    disturbed, as defect, 89, 91-2
    fingerprints on, 29
    original (OG), 29
Gutter pair (G/PR), 139

H

Handling stamps, 53-60
Handstamped (HS or H/S), 139
Harmers of New York, Inc., 21
Heavily cancelled (HC), 139
Heavily hinged (HH), 139
Herst, Jr., Herman, 92, 132
Highway Post Office (HPO), 139
Hill, Rowland, 79
Hinge remnants (HR), 139
Hinged (H), 139
Hinges, stamp, 55-7
History of the Postage Stamps of the United States, The, 133
Hitler stamps, 84
Humidifying boxes, 55
Hunting Permit Stamps, 65

I

Imperforate (IMPERF), 139
Imperforate errors, 99
Inaugural covers, 52
Ink eradicator, 93
Insurance for stamp collections, 118

Internal Revenue Service, 39
International Philatelic Exhibition, 36
Inverted (INVT), 139
Investing in stamps, 105-119
    air mail, 112
    appreciation is never guaranteed, 115
    as compared with other investments, 111
    best to buy quality, 118
    factors affecting, 105
    first-day covers, 112-3
    from telemarketing firm, 114-5
    Graf Zeppelins, 115
    long-term market trends, 106-7
    market cycles, 105-6
    overpaying, 111-2
    plate blocks, 114
    price cycles, 111
    U.S. Columbian Exposition stamps, 113-4
Investment stamps, which ones to buy, 110-1
Israeli stamps (first), 85

J

J. Nalbandian, Inc., 100
Jacques C. Schiff, Jr., Inc., 100
Johl, Max G., 132

K

Kehr, Ernest A., 132
Kennedy topicals, 83
King, Beverly S., 132

L

Left, right (L, R), 139
Leonard H. Hartmann, 131
Lightly cancelled (LC), 139
Lightly hinged (LH), 139
Line pair (LP or L/P), 139
Linn's Stamp News, 14, 132
Linn, George, 47
Local, 139
Local posts, 39-40
Los Angeles Olympics Stamps, 66

Los Angeles Times, 15
Loso, Foster W., 132
Lower left/lower right (LL/LR), 139
Luff, John N., 132
Luminescent stamps, 69

M

Magnifiers, 58
Mail bid sales, 22
Manuscript (MS), 140
Margin (MRGN), 140
Marginal inscription (MI), 140
Market cycles for investors, 105-6
Market trends, long-term, 106-7
Market value, factors that affect, 107-8
Marvin Frey, 100
Military covers, 41, 43-5
    prices, 45
Minor defect (MD), 140
Mint (M), 140
Mint, never hinged (MNH), 140
Mint and unused stamps, differences between, 29-30
Mint stamps, 29-30
    in sheets (panes), 109-110
Mis-registered color errors, 103
Misperforated (MISPERF), 140
Misrepresentation, 89
"Mission Mixtures", 122
Mixtures of stamps, 13-4
    sample packets, 14
Mueller, Barbara R., 132
Multiple, 140
Museum stamp exhibits, 123

N

Nassau Street, 132
National Parks, 63-4
National Tuberculosis Association, 35
Never hinged (NH), 29, 140
New York Herald Tribune, 132
New Zealand Expeditions, 83-4
Newspaper stamp columns, 15
NH (never hinged), 29
No gum (NG), 140

O

1-cent Z-Grill, 73
Obsolete, 140
Off center, 140
Off paper, 140
Omnibus issues, 86-7
Original Gum (OG), 29, 140
    never hinged (OGNH), 91
Other uses of stamps, 121-4
Overpaying for stamps, 111-2
Overprint (OVPT), 140
Overprints and surcharges, 40

P

Pair (PR), 140
Pan-Americans, 63
Pane, 141
"Paper chase, the", 19
Paper preservation and restoration, 93
Parcel Posts, 64-5
Pat Paragraphs, 133
Perfection, beware of, 92
Perforated initials (PERFINS or PI's), 141
Perforation (PERF), 141
Perforations, damaged, 92
Perry, Elliott, 133
Philatelic Catalog, 19
Philatelic covers, 41-2
Philatelic Foundation Certificate (PFC), 141
Philatelic Foundation, 78, 130
Philatelic homework, essential for investors, 105
Philatelic Sales Division (U.S. Postal Service), 19
Philatelic supply dealers, 55
Philatelic Trader's Society (PTS), 141
Philatelic Use, 141
Philatelic weeklies, 25-6
Philately, 141
"Pigeon Post" mail, 47
Pinholes, 89, 90-1
    effect on market value, 90
Planty, Earl, 133
Plate block (PB), 141

Plate blocks, 20, 31, 114, 125-6
    as investments, 114
    increasing cost of collecting, 125-6
Plate number (PL NO or PL#), 141
Plate smears, 99
Playing card stamps, 39
Pony Express, 40, 71
Pony Express covers, 41
Popular stamps, U.S., 61-3
    air mails, 64
    Columbians, 61-3
    national parks, 63-4
    Pan-Americans, 63
    presidentials, 64
    Trans-Mississippians, 63
Post card (PC or P/C), 141
Post cards vs. postal cards, 34-5
Post cards, World War I, 47
Post Office Department (POD), (U.S.), 64, 142
Postage Currency, Civil War, 71-2
Postage due (PD), 141
Postage due stamps, 33-4
Postage Stamps of the United States, 132
Postal Card (PC or P/C also), 141
Postal Cards errors, 102
Postal cards vs. post cards, 34-5
Postal Guide to U.S. Stamps, The, 19
Postal history, 141
Postal Service (U.S.), 19-20, 24, 31, 34, 36, 50, 74, 102
    Domestic Mail Manual, 48
    issuing too many stamps?, 125
    Philatelic Sales Division, 19
Postal Service of the Confederate States of America, The, 132
Postal stationery, 142
Postmark (PMK), 142
Precancel (PREC), 142
Presidentials, 64
Price cycles, 111
Price on Request (P.O.R.), 119
Prices, wholesale and retail, 108

Printing runs, average for U.S. stamps, 68
Proof (P or PR or PRF), 142
Public libraries, books on stamps, 14-5

R

Ragsdale Stamp Company, 20
Railway Post Office (RPO), 142
Rare cancels, 51
Rare finds, 22-3
Rare stamps, 23-4, 71-8, 97
    errors, 97
    searching for, 23-4
    U.S., 71-8
Reasons for collecting stamps, 13
Regummed (RG), 142
Reprint (R), 142
Revenue stamps, 37
Revenues, U.S., 72-3
    playing card, 72
Robert A. Siegel Auction Galleries, 20
Romance of Stamp collecting, The, 132
Roulette (R), 142
Russian stamps, 84-5
Rust spots, 90

S

Safe deposit boxes, 93, 118
Safes, for storing stamps, 58-9
Sanitary Fairs, 68
Scheele, Carl H., 133
Scott Catalog Value (SCV), 142
Scott catalogs, 14
Scott Publishing Company, 109
Se-tenant, 143
Seals, Christmas, 35
Selvage (SEL or SELV), 142
Semi-postal, 142
Semi-postal stamps, 35-6
Separation (SEP), 142
Set, 142
Sheet, 143
Short History of the Mail Service, A, 133
Short perforation (SH PF), 143
Sleeper, 143

Sloane's Columns, 133
Sloane, George B., 133
Soaking stamps, 53-4
   when not to, 54
Society sales circuits, 27
Sources of stamps, 19-27
Souvenir cards, 36
Souvenir sheet (SS or S/S), 143
Souvenir sheets, 36
Space Covers, 41, 50-1
Space filler, 143
Special cancels, 48
Special delivery stamps, 33
Specialized collecting, 66-8
Specialties, 29, 87
   British Commonwealth, 87
   collecting, 29
Specimen (S), 143
Speculators, as investors, 106
Stains, 89-90
Stamp books, in public libraries, 14-5
Stamp books, where to buy, 15
Stamp bourse, 24
Stamp categories, 29-40
Stamp clubs, 15-6
Stamp collecting, future of, 125-130
Stamp collecting, specialties, 29
Stamp Collector, 14
Stamp Collectors' Round Table, The, 132
Stamp columns in newspapers, 15
Stamp dealers, 24-6
Stamp donations, 121-2
   possible tax benefits, 121
   to libraries and museums, 123
Stamp hinges, 55-7
   gum disturbance from, 57
Stamp shops, 19, 20
   "bid boards", 20
Stamp shows, 24-6
Stamp tagging, 69
Stamp tongs, 55
Stamp weeklies, 14
Stampless covers, 51-2, 143
Stamps, "Duck", 37-8
Stamps, 14, 133

Stamps, 105-119
   air mail, 30
   as decorations, 122
   as donations to libraries and museums, 123
   as donations to non-profit organizations, 121-2
   as historical objects, 13
   as prizes, 122-3
   as teaching aids, 124
   Australian "Roos", 80
   average printing runs, 68
   British Commonwealth specialties, 87
   buying through classified ads, 26-7
   Canadian, early, 80-1
   Canal Zone, 69-70
   cancelled, 30
   cancels, 36
   categories of, 29-40
      air mails, 29
      commemoratives, 29
      definitives, 29
      souvenir sheets, 29
   classifications, 29
   cleaning and repairing (ethics of), 89, 94
   Columbian reissues, 127-8
   Danish, 85
   demonitized, 68-99
   encased, 77-8
   errors, 97-104
   Falkland Islands, 86
   foreign, 79-87
      inexpensive beginner kits, 79
   German cancels (rare), 84
   germs on, 58
   getting started, 11-7
   government saving, 38
   Great Britain, early, 79-80
   handling, 53
      tools, 53
   historical value, 33
   Hitler, 84
   investing in, 105-119
   Israeli (first), 85
   Kennedy topicals, 83
   local posts, 39-40

Stamps, cont.
   Luminescent, 69
   mint, 29-30
      in sheets (panes), 109-110
   mixtures of, 13-4
   New Zealand Expeditions, 83-4
   omnibus issues, 86-7
   other uses of, 121-4
   playing card, 39
   postage due, 33-4
   rare, searching for, 23-4
   revenue, 37
   Russian, 84-5
   Sanitary Fair, 68
   semi-postal, 35-6
   soaking, 53-4
      when not to, 54
   sources of, 19-27
   special delivery, 33
   telegraph, 38-9
   topical, 34
   U.S., most popular, 61-4
   U.S., need for improved quality control, 126
   U.S., new subjects for, 126-7
   U.S., quality of modern printing, 126
   U.S. collectors, 12
   U.S. Hunting Permit, 36-7
   U.S. Postal Savings, 38
   U.S. rare, 71-8
      $5 definitives, 73-4
      1-cent Z-Grill, 73
      1847 issues, 75
      Confederate States Postmasters' Provisionals, 75-6
      Graf Zeppelins, 74
   United Nations, 70
   United States, 61-70
      rare, 71-8
   unused, 29-30
   used, 30
   where to find, 19-28
Stamps for the Wounded, 121
Stanley Gibbons Stamp Catalogue, The, 83
Stanton, Thomas, 133

Starting in stamps, 11-7
Storage, 118
Storage, 58-60
    effects of environment, 59-60
    safe deposit boxes, 59
    safes, 58
Straight edge (SE or S/E), 143
Stuck sheets, problems in separating, 54-5
Superb (SUP or S), 143
Superior Stamp & Coin Company, 21, 73
Supply and demand, effect on market value, 107-8
Surcharge, 143
Surcharges and overprints, 40
Swap meets, 19

T

2-cent Columbian, 66
Teaching with stamps, 124
Tear (TR), 143
Telegraph stamps, 38-9
Telemarketing stamp sales, be suspicious of, 114-5
Tete-beche, 43
"Thematics", 34
Thin (TH), 143
Thorp, Prescott H., 133
Thorp-Bartels Catalogue of United States Stamped Envelopes, The, 133
Three Cent Stamp of the United States, The, 131
Tied on, 144
Tied to piece (TTP), 144
Tiffany, John K., 133

Tiny (T), 144
Tongs, stamp, 55
Top/bottom (T/B), 144
Topical stamps, 34
Topicals, 144
Trans-Missisippians, 63
Turner, George, 133

U

U.S. Columbian Exposition Stamps, as investments, 113-4
U.S. Parcel Post: A Postal History, 65
U.S. Philatelic Classics Society, 24
U.S. Postal Inspection Service, 92
U.S. Revenues, 72-3
    playing card, 72
U.S. Specialized Catalog (Scott's), 31
United Nations Postal Administration, 70
United Nations stamps, 70
United States First Day Cover Catalog of Classic Cachets, 133
United States One Cent Stamp of 1851-1857, The, 131
United States Postage Stamps — How to Collect, Understand, and Enjoy Them, 132
United States Postage Stamps of the Nineteenth Century, The, 131, 132
United States Postal Service (USPS), 144
United States stamps, 61-70
    rare, 71-8

Unlisted (UNL), 144
Unused (UN), 144
Unused stamps, 29-30
Upper left/upper right (UL/UR), 144
Used (U), 144
Used stamps, 30

V

Variety (VAR), 144
Very fine (VF), 144
Very good (VG), 144
Very lightly hinged (VLH), 144
Vignette, 144

W

Walcott, George, 133
Wallpaper, 145
War Cover Club, 24
Watermark (WMK), 145
Watermark errors, 103-4
Weeklies, philatelic, 25-6
Wells Fargo, 40
Western Union Telegraph Company, 39
Where to find stamps, 19-28
Wholesale and retail prices, difference between, 108
Williams, L. N., 134
Williams, M., 134
With/without (W or W/O), 145
World War I post cards, 47
Worldwide collections, 85-6

Y

"Your Stamps", 15